ODDYSSEY

TERESA RENDA CARLSON

3 SWALLYS PRESS
BOSTON

Copyright © 2020 by Teresa Renda Carlson
Cover design and interior illustrations by Paul Trainor
All rights reserved

Originally written in Italian by Teresa Renda Carlson, and translated to English by the author herself.

Paperback ISBN 978-0-9987651-1-2

1. Memoir. 2. Italy–History–1942–1959

To the women of Capistrano, including my family, who nourished me when hungry with their bodies, and their warmth and love.

And to my Julian, whose unfailing constancy in playing the cello helped me to come out of this selva oscura.

Contents

ACKNOWLEDGMENTS	1
PROLOGUE	3
1. MY VILLAGE	6
2. SERRA SAN BRUNO	15
3. THE BIRTH	20
4. THE RESCUE	28
5. THE FORBIDDEN JOURNEY	34
6. MY FIRST BRUSH WITH DEATH	39
7. THE PROCESSION	48
8. BACK TO SERRA SAN BRUNO	53
9. SHALL I OR SHALL I NOT…	58
10. SUSU	60
11. MY LAST DAY IN CAPISTRANO	76
12. CHIAZZARELLO	85
13. THE LADY DRESSED IN BLACK	98
14. AN EPIC VOYAGE	103
15. THE ESCAPE	115
16. A TRAGEDY	118
17. MY MATERNAL GRANDPARENTS	129
18. THE ARRIVAL	147
EPILOGUE: A GENTLE DEATH	159

Acknowledgments

I would like to thank my husband and daughter Licia for reading the first draft; my grandson Julian Carlson Frank for the pictures of Capistrano and others; and James Florio for giving me the picture of Arridavota with his family.

Prologue

I came into the world among discord, terror and disappointment, under a bridge that was ready to fall and become another testimony to the destruction of a war in 1942, when the world went crazy and lost its equilibrium.

At the critical age of seventeen, I left my adored village for Canada, a land as foreign to me as Mars, on a ship called Vulcania on her last voyage to then retire into oblivion. But before leaving, a couple of days before, I had to come to terms with my own identity, a search that began early in my life.

Whenever I saw a group of little ladies I would sit there and listen to their stories of births and miscarriages, hoping that they would talk about my birth, a subject that everyone avoided, including my parents. My sister Nina, then an eight-year-old, found delight in telling me how she would bravely go from house to house, begging the ladies who had newborn babies to nurse me, and if they refused, she would try to bribe them with a bottle of olive oil. She knew how to barter, a skill very much practiced in our village.

I did not want to leave my world, yet I had no choice; the Oracle at Delphi had spoken... my father, the paterfamilias par excellence, commanded it. I had no choice but to obey and listen to the Atlantic sirens, calling me to a bigger world far away, where even my imagination did not want to go. I was too deeply embedded in my little village, which offered me, yes, a primitive life, but rich in oral history, Latin and Greek culture.

I learned so much every day, though I did not attend school for many years. How I loved the evenings when, all huddled near the brazier full of flaming charcoal (keeping the front of you roasted but your back cold as ice) we waited for that knock at the door when Mastro Antonio would come to perform opera. He knew most operas by heart and would sing them after telling the intricate and violent stories of betrayal, death and duels, which would have scared us if not for the glorious melodies that clothed them. Carmen is killed at the end of the opera, and yet we would be humming the "Toreador Song" all evening. What was it in music that elevated the soul beyond any terrestrial mishap? I would ask questions that irritated Mastro Antonio like, "Why are the women killed most of the time?" I heard only admonitions to keep quiet and listen, or the maestro would unleash his cane on me. How did he

PROLOGUE

know all these operas? I would weave my own stories.

Mastro Antonio was not only human but also divine; he had descended to Earth from Mount Olympus to sing to us, to take our minds off the war that was raging like a monster ready to devour everything and everyone. He was the god of music, Orpheus, who, desperate for having left behind his beloved Eurydice in the underworld, came back to Earth and inhabited the body of a simple villager, our Mastro Antonio.

How I loved my little village; my heart ached at the thought of leaving it, and it would continue to ache more and more through the many memories built through the years. I was consoled by the fact that I had lived consciously the many aspects of village life, savoring every moment, be it good or bad. I convinced myself that one day I would come back. I would leave my abode as a young girl and come back as a mature woman.

1

My Village

Nestled in a valley surrounded by mountains and sea like a baby in a cradle, a little village emerges in the soft light of dawn from its slumber to its immutable and arcane rhythm of life, only to slowly melt into the sunset and lose itself once again in the immensity of the night. Immersed in its sleep, it dreams of a brighter tomorrow, unaware of the deafening sounds of the airplanes flying over it, throwing luminous flares in search of it. Fortunately, the flares fall in the gorge that runs along the outside of the village, creating a protective barrier, and the airplanes fly away, certain that nothing exists beyond the gorge; the village is saved once again, at least for another night.

At sunrise, at the sound of the church bells, the village arises once more to its jubilant people, to its houses huddled together as in a prayer, to its narrow, serpentine cobblestone roads which, like rivulets, wind down toward the greater sea—the piazza—a small Romanesque structure dominated by a niche in which resides a statue of the Madonna of the Mountains, who, marmoreal in her alcove above the main entrance, remains always vigilant and faithful to her village and its people.

The church of the Madonna of the Mountains, Capistrano

Inside the church, in an ornate gold gilded niche on the main altar, sits another majestic statue of the Madonna of the Mountains, patiently listening to the invocations of the people. She is a celestial vision of beauty and serenity: luminous blue eyes, angelic face, blond curly hair cascading down on her shoulders, which imperially support a long white neck, the neck of a ballerina, and a head on which sits a golden crown bejeweled with rubies, garnets and emeralds shedding light around her already luminous face. Her clothes are made of Renaissance brocades embroidered by the nimble hands of the nuns. On her lap stands baby Jesus, equally radiantly attired, holding in his right hand a blue ball representing the universe.

The legend goes that a long time ago, before cars were invented and people used horses and carriages, Auguste Renoir allegedly passed by our village, and in return for hospitality, painted two frescoes in the baptistry: one, the Baptism of Jesus, and the other, too ruined to identify the subject matter (historians to this day dispute the identity of the painter and the authenticity of the frescoes, but very little is absolute truth in this village—reality changes as the light that bathes it and gives it life).

The story continues that a group of robbers came to the procession of the Madonna. The feast, which is celebrated every year on the second Sunday of August, is the only time the Madonna leaves her domain, and she is carried by the men through the entire village in a royal procession. The band, usually local, accompanies the Madonna by playing Verdi's and Rossini's marches and many sacred hymns, which the women sing with great ardor, fervor and devotion, and with deep, velvety but dissonant voices. The children, elegantly dressed, jubilantly walk in front of the Madonna, carrying baskets of flower petals still pearled with dew, throwing them on the cobblestone roads to decorate the way, as if the Madonna herself had descended from her throne and walked on the fresh petals.

Every balcony is covered with colorful and embroidered silks, woven on the loom by the women. The Madonna stops in front of the houses of the more distinguished inhabitants, and the band plays a special piece to thank them for their generous contributions to the church. The robbers' eyes glistened, like newly fallen snow bathed by the rays of the sun, at the sight of all that money, and they patiently continued to be in the procession, notwithstanding the sweltering heat.

Once the Madonna reentered the church at the sound of the "Triumphal March" of the opera *Aida*, she was safely placed on a table covered with a cloth, not only woven by the hands of some women of the parish, but decorated with the finest embroidery of the flora of the place; the fields, too, came to greet our Madonna. Everyone, exhausted but proud, walked home, where a sumptuous meal that would last for hours would be served, accompanied by the *vino locale*, a specialty of every household. Most villagers would save up all year for this meal; the feast of the Madonna was perhaps the most expensive endeavor of the year.

The robbers, well aware of the habits of the villagers, decided to wait patiently under the acacia trees, eating and drinking the food and the wine that was brought to them by some generous villagers, even though they had refused to join them in their abodes. They had other plans.

"How shy and discreet they are, they do not want to intrude, and how devotedly they did the whole procession, they must love our Madonna," the women would ingeniously say as they rejoined their banquets.

After a couple of hours, when they were sure the wine had taken its effect on the people, the robbers went to the church and began to lift the Madonna and carry her outside, where a cart and two somnolent horses were waiting. But the Madonna became so heavy and unmovable that after Herculean efforts, sweat dripping from their brows like the fountain in the piazza, after many imprecations that would have made the devil blush, they decided to abandon their plans. The Madonna had spoken; she was happy with her little village, its immutable rhythm of life and death, untouched by the world beyond, so it seemed.

The robbers left in search of other Madonnas, perhaps live ones this time. I heard many stories of beautiful women who were kidnapped by the men who loved them. One story I found most intricate was told to me by the lady herself who, one evening on her way home from the fields, was pulled up by a man on a white horse, and they both galloped toward the man's home, where his mother was waiting for them. The woman's parents went to the house where their daughter was kept prisoner; the daughter came to the balcony and told them to return home; there was nothing they could do for her, for her wings were clipped and she could no longer fly. The parents understood immediately and, desperately embracing the truth, left. The man married her and they had seven happy and beautiful children who grew to love their dad, who, in spite of his horrible act, turned out to be a loving and caring man to his family. When I heard this story, I was glad I was ugly, for certainly no one would pull me away from my family. "*Non tutti i mali non vengono per nuocere*"; not all bad things come to harm us.

This custom reminded me of Il Ratto di Polissena, whose statue is in the Piazza della Signoria, in Florence. Mastro Antonio, on one of his trips to Florence, bought a miniature of it and, like a magician, he would pull it out from his pocket and show it to us. I wanted to touch it and hold it, but as magically as it appeared, it disappeared into another of his labyrinthian pockets. I was glad I was not Polissena either, one of the Sabine women, not that anyone would kidnap me; all the women of the village thought I was ugly and did not miss any occasion to tell me so. I was glad to be ugly and to live in my village, where robbers wanted only Madonnas and beautiful women.

In my village if a man loved a woman, he would go under her balcony, if she had one, and serenade her by playing guitar and singing love songs. One starry night a group of suitors came under our balcony to sing to one of my older sisters, which one we did not know, for they were all beautiful. It had to be for one of them; I was only a little girl, and ugly at that. Guitar in hand they began to sing a rather nasty song. I, quietly like a mouse, got up, crept to the window in the dark, and by the light of a harvest moon was able to identify them. One of the troubadours was in love with my second sister, Pina, whose face was as luminous as the moon. Pina hated this man with a passion. Suddenly, a small figure approached the window. I hid under the dining room table. She gently opened the finestra and poured a chamber pot full to the brim with the nectar of its goddesses onto the troubadours' wide-open mouths at the height of their nasty words. They ran away into the darkness, howling like mad wounded wolves, never to be heard again. My mother knew how to take care of them.

Unfortunately for the little village, the planes in search of it did come back, and their rumbling sound echoed through the valleys and the hills around and beyond. The bells of the church desperately and continuously rang their song of alarm. The sound was different from the customary one of death, which was the only thing constant in this village. They rang three times for a man, two for a child and one for a woman. Even the bells seemed to know the patriarchal order of things. I was amazed.

The bells had no intention of stopping; their shrill sound piercing through the night like a spear woke the slumberous inhabitants who, like blind bats, moved around not knowing where to go: to the ravine, to the mountains or toward the sound of the bells, to the piazza, to the church.

Most seemed to go toward the church, whose doors were wide open like the mouth of a whale ready to swallow them into its vortex. The people arrived there in throngs, squealing like baby seals, and began to pray sotto voce to the Madonna to protect them and their village from the ravages of a war they did not understand.

It was a very dark night; the darkness swallowed everyone and everything, even the voices of the people who, exhausted by their constant invocations for protection, fell asleep on the marble pavement of the church. It was during one of these nights, as I was about to find out, that I was born.

2

Serra San Bruno

Zia Maria came down from her upstairs house, and the two of us left for Serra San Bruno. I was full of hope that something magical would happen, my second-to-last day in this blessed land. Being with Zia Maria was always magical to me; there was something ethereal, untouchable, that united us, that made our hearts sing when

Zia Maria (back left), Teresa's mother Angela (middle), Teresa (right), with Maria's children, Ciccio, Enzo, Gigi, and Nina, all wearing clothes received from the Marshall Plan, summer 1958

we were together. I loved her voice as it surged from her cavernous being into the heavens, making them smile; her beautiful hands when she prayed seemed to touch divinity.

She and I went alone to visit the Certosa of Serra San Bruno, to relive perhaps for the last time the events that took place on this blessed ground, and to thank San Bruno for the protection he offered us during the war years. San Bruno, too, left his beloved France and a wonderful career in the church to become a hermit in the mountains of Calabria, among the tall and majestic beech trees. In vain the Pope summoned him to Rome; he listened instead to the call he heard in his heart.

Arm in arm, we climbed into the bus and our mini voyage began. We felt the excitement in our bodies as the bus left with a lion's roar, and we looked into each other's dark eyes and let their warmth caress our wounded souls. How hard it seemed to me to abandon one's roots for an uncertain and faraway land, where the language, the basis of communication, would sound like noises; each syllable running one into the other, creating a cacophony of discordant sounds to my untrained ear. I learned later that until one begins to distinguish syllables, everything appears to be garbled up. Was I up to the challenge?

The sudden rocking of the bus broke my reverie, and Zia Maria handed me a panino. We had only been in the bus for an hour and we were already eating. "Mangia, mangia, il pane l'ho fatto io." (Eat, eat, I made the bread.)

SERRA SAN BRUNO

I could not say no to her, even though my stomach was queasy. I took it from her hand, and for the first time I did not gulp it down. I was a war child, and food was always welcomed. Zia Maria fell asleep, and I was left alone to the sound of the bus and to my queasy stomach, thinking of the only thing I was able to think of those days, my little village. I succumbed to its spell and fell asleep.

I woke up in Serra San Bruno. We walked off the bus and went to the little lake and prayed silently in front of the statue of San Bruno, which stood silently and in prayer in the holy, miraculous waters of the lake.

Lake in Serra San Bruno with statue of San Bruno in the water, where he prayed daily

Then we went toward the big cement steps that lead to the monastery. Zia Maria took my hand and led me toward them.

With measured and steady steps, with certainty and familiarity of having done it before, hand in hand, in reverent silence, we climbed the stairway leading to the monastery. A gentle, soothing warmth transferred from her hand to mine. How I loved that hand—callous, strong, decisive, familiar to the many she helped, gentle to the children she caressed, a hand which on a moonless night, brought to her bosom a wisp of flesh that had just been born in the darkness, born to fear, to despair, in the faint light of a moribund oil lamp.

My hand, in contrast to hers, was smooth, weak, feeble, a hand not yet chiseled by the vicissitudes of life—a hand that could not let go of the warmth the other hand emanated, the energy it infused into my being, my tortured being, afraid of the impending departure to a world far, far away, where children, I was told, watched television and ate cereal in front of it.

An inner silence permeated our bodies and silenced our lips but not our hearts, which still felt the horror of that night, that horrible night when enemy planes encircled and deafened our world. The monastery, which miraculously survived, remained the ever-present symbol of our hope for a better tomorrow by tirelessly and silently listening to our anguishes and struggles—a silent participant in a world in chaos.

We continued our climb in perfect harmony, although a cauldron of anguish was brewing inside my apprehensive being (in two days I would go away from this blessed place). As we climbed higher and higher, our memories, untiring custodians of our identities, were emerging from hibernation like wild animals ready to be heard and disrupt the serenity of the morning. We stopped our climb, our eyes met, mine imploring, perhaps for the last time, to hear the story of my *essere o non essere* (being or not being). She quickly understood—many times before had she seen those dark, imploring eyes. She beckoned me to sit on the second-to-last step. She pulled out one of her long sighs from her being as easily as a magician pulls out a rabbit from a hat, took a deep breath, and with great devotion to the narrative, began her "Miserere," her story, with the serenity and humility of a nun at Vespers.

3

The Birth

"It was a moonless night; the darkness swallowed everything and everyone except the sound of the bells and the faint sound of a young woman who was trying to expel from her tired, scared and malnourished body her seventh child, hoping against hope that this time it would be a boy. A faint smile of hope caressed her parched lips and lighted the pallor of her face as she was carried like the Madonna from her house to what they thought a more secure place. She was followed by her own little procession, her children, her husband, her father, her brother-in-law and the midwife. The only cover available to them, as their minds scrambled in confusion, was the bridge near the oil refinery, *il frantoio*, her father had built before the war. The *frantoio* was a repository of happy memories. The river nearby would provide the water necessary and a place to dispose of the placenta. An oil lamp, faintly and trembling by the hurriedness of the pace, lighted the way

THE BIRTH

as they walked on the cobblestones toward the gentle, almost inaudible hymn of the river.

"Once there, a blanket was spread on the grassy riverbank under the bridge, where the woman (parturient) lay down to do the work that only women do, to bring out this blessed boy who one day would be the protector of his sisters and chase away the unworthy suitors. But the little 'boy' was not in any hurry to leave the secure, warm abode of the womb for a less secure, chaotic, war-ravaged place. After all, this was 1942, when the world went mad, mad, mad—a long night of madness which lasted till 1945.

"The woman's white lips gave a faint smile. She was a strong woman, familiar to labor pains. The midwife sat close to her, ready to catch the baby, but fervently praying that a bomb would not truncate her young life before she was able to consummate her ardent love for the brother-in-law of the parturient. She hoped she would be married and have her own children. She longed to be a mother, a wife... but most of all now she longed to hold the hand of her beloved, who, by her side, was groping in the dark for hers. He wanted to keep her hands warm to receive the new creature, if he ever decided to come. The children whimpered softly but steadily in their sleep. They were hungry and cold. They had to leave their warm, soft beds and abandon their sweet dreams, in which the rumbling airplanes became white swans, wings spread, floating above their beds, emitting from their bodies white chocolate eggs. The youngest, two years old, was now crying. Her father picked her up and held her close to his heart, which was galloping at the idea of holding his soon-to-be little boy.

" 'Quiet, quiet, in a little while your little brother will come.' But the little girl had no intention of stopping. She did not want a little brother, but a white chocolate egg instead. 'When is my boy coming, *Signorina*? Be careful to catch him well, that he does not fall on the ground,' forgetting that his wife was already lying on the ground. 'Wretched lantern, it died—now, yes, we risk losing him in this evil darkness.'

"The *signorina* [midwife] sweetly took away the hand of her beloved from her breast, and with tremendous and burning lips, barely able to formulate the words: 'Patience, patience, I am not God almighty—it takes time to bring a boy into the world—it is not an egg, you know.'

" 'Where is my chocolate egg?' shouted the little girl, sleeping on her father's chest.

" 'Here, here is your baby, he is coming out,' announced the *signorina*, as if all the merit was hers.

"The father quickly put the little girl on the blanket, grabbed the little creature from the midwife's hand with a brutal force not unlike that of the wind that tears the nascent leaves off the branches of a budding tree, and with trepidation exposed the baby's genitals to the tremulous light of the lantern, almost extinguished by that rapid

THE BIRTH

movement. An exasperated, anguished, shrill sound came from his big chest.

" '*Merda*, what have you done! It is a girl, another girl! But then you don't understand anything, *Signorina*; where is your head?!'

" 'Excuse me! It is the lantern's fault, it was dying. It has nothing to do with me. My duty is to help children come into the world, your world of *merda*, and not to make them male or female—that's your job, not mine,' she said miffed, confounded and scared.

"The silence of the grave enveloped everyone; even the river seemed to have stopped its perpetual song. Everyone was exhausted by the long wait. Suddenly, a hushed cry was heard; a sorrowful, guilty cry. It was the silent cry of the mother, saddened and disappointed by the birth of another girl. She was guilty of not being able to give her man a little boy, a boy who would have given name and security to the family. The words of Auntie Filomena buzzed in her head like a bunch of thirsty bees: 'Where there is no man, there is no name.' She had her man; a strong man at that, but she would have been happy to give him a companion to go hunting with. Instead, he was surrounded by women, only women. Did she have the strength to weave more blankets, sheets, and more tomatoes and beans to plant? Food was scarce—as if boys did not need to eat; she did not make sense. Desperate and feverish, she took the baby and threw her to the end of the blanket. The baby, fragile, skeleton-like, without emitting a sound, fixed her two black olive eyes on the devastated face of the mother. The moon, with her luminous and silvery face, appeared and shed her light on that skeletal face, dominated by the two enormous black eyes. The mother felt remorseful, but exhausted and defeated, abandoned herself to the misery of being a woman, a mother, a wife, and a victim of a war raging inside and out.

"Everything became dark again. The moon stopped lighting the opaque faces, the lantern stopped being a lantern, her flame forever extinguished like the hope of that poor mother to bring into the world a baby boy. Everyone abandoned themselves to the sadness of the moment, a moment that seemed endless, until a figure appeared in the penumbra."

We slowly and quietly got up, as if we did not want to break that spell, and climbed the last step, both moved by that incredible tale; she more resolute to continue, to finally release that doleful story to the elements, after seventeen years of keeping it buried in the secret chambers of her being; to expose it to the light of my memory so that time would not destroy it once she was no longer with us.

"*Ricordare e' vivere—Narrare e' ricordare*" (to remember is to live—to narrate is to remember), she whispered to me as she looked sweetly and tenderly into my eyes. "Soon you will leave me," she said as she fixed her disheveled hair and sat down on the last step, and without further delay, she continued her tale.

"A white figure appeared in the heart of the night to our little group still under the bridge, each resigned to his or her fate, listening to the never-ending lullaby of the river, which, while still oblivious to their anguish, managed to help the children fall into a deep sleep. Dawn would soon arise and disclose the ghostly presence, enlighten the heart of the new mother and envelop her in a mantle of resignation and hope; the hope which, even under the worst circumstances, a new life brings forth. The ghostly figure became more visible to the group, and the children recognized her as Suor Pie Marie, their aunt, their beloved nun.

" 'In the name of God, what are all you doing here, and under a bridge of all places,' uttered Suor Pie Marie in astonishment.

" 'The Germans threw a flair in the sky, and it fortunately fell in the ravine, and seeing nothing worthwhile to bomb, they left. The little town is safe for another day,' said Nonno Luigi.

" 'Don't you know a bridge is the most dangerous place to be under?'

" 'We had no choice, your sister decided to…' yelled Nonno with indignation. Then a whimpering cry was heard.

"'Who is crying?'

"'She is our new baby!' yelled out the girls jubilantly.

"The poor baby could find no peace; she was hungry and, with difficulty, she tried to bring her little hand to her mouth. The mother tried and tried to bring her to her breast, but without success—nothing was coming from her breasts. She was in a state of shock and the fear of a bomb falling on them had caused her colostrum to dry up. There was absolutely nothing they could give her. Someone needed to go out and find a wet nurse, but who dared to leave the refuge with the airplanes still rumbling overhead. Even the bells were afraid to ring, now that the faint light of dawn was disclosing the village. Fortunately, a thick fog descended, and it swallowed everyone and everything as voraciously as a shark swallows its prey. Everyone breathed a sigh of relief, except the new baby, who continued her deafening squeal like the cicadas that, having nothing else to do, abandon themselves to their annoying songs and then are heard no more. Not knowing what else to do, Suor Pie Marie took the little creature from the limp arms of the mother and brought her to her breast, hugging and lullabying her. Her little heart was beating strongly and regularly, like Nonno's watch, and continued beating as if a magical hand had wound it up. Her heart had its work to do too; it had a specific purpose to keep that wisp of flesh alive.

"But the baby continued to cry with new vigor now,

THE BIRTH

and with a constancy that surpassed that of the cicadas. It went on and on without any intention of stopping until her needs were met. Crying was her duty; it announced to the world and to all that she was hungry and cold. Suor Pie Marie took out from her huge habit pocket an Italian flag, the only possession she was able to carry with her as the bombs fell on her convent in France. She carefully wrapped the baby in it, hoping that the piercing cry would stop and give everyone a moment of peace. But the baby went on and on. All of a sudden, the cry stopped, and everyone felt relieved and abandoned themselves to that mystical peace that the fog brought.

4

The Rescue

"But the peace did not last long; the deafening cry resumed. Nonno, no longer able to hear that familiar piercing sound, stretched his gigantic hand toward that cry and placed it on the baby's mouth. That sorrowful cry was also swallowed by the fog, and everything was peaceful again. Suor Pie Marie quickly understood what had happened, and like lightning, grabbed Nonno's hand and bit it away. Like a lioness, with incredible speed, she left the den, carrying her baby to safety; she continued her flight for a long time and stopped only when she heard the gentle hymn of the river, the same river but farther up the hills. She was now too far from the bridge. Exhausted, she fell on the grass, which, having been kissed by the morning dew, provided a refreshing respite. A ray of sun pierced through the fog and lit the baby's face; she hugged her to her breast and the two hearts started to beat in unison. They were both alive and well, but the little body could not stop trembling like a new leaf touched by the wind of life for the first time. She took off her cape and wrapped her in it, and having nothing else to offer her, she put her finger on the baby's mouth and began to sing her favorite lullaby, 'Fait doh doh,' in a soft and gentle voice so as not to wake up God's creation. Both were soon enveloped in a deep sleep, and she was feverish, but happy that she had arrived in time to save her little one from the desperate hand of grandpa.

" 'How ugly war is; it makes savages of us all,' she muttered and abandoned herself to the fog and to the melodious song of the river, which, notwithstanding the war, continued on its course, singing its hymn of joy.

"Dawn was now in full bloom. A sunray touched Suor Pie Marie's lips with its balmy warmth, and her mouth immediately opened like a tulip to the "Salve Regina," the hymn she was accustomed to recite first thing in the morning in the Carmelite convent, together with the other sisters. She finished her morning prayers and looked down toward her breast, and she saw the baby sucking at her breast with zest and gusto like a hungry cub. Amazed and awe-struck, she pulled the suckling away from her breast, and colostrum, a grayish, sticky liquid, was trickling out of her nipple like an ornamental fountain. She placed the baby back to her breast, and the little creature continued her work with new zeal and agility. She had mastered the art of sucking. Suor Pie Marie abandoned herself to that miracle.

"A miracle it was. How could those skeletal little hands have been able to unbutton and go through the layers of those complicated nunnery habits? She felt reborn and almost ecstatic, and sotto voce, not to disturb her little cub, began to sing the 'Magnificat.'

" '*Magnificat, magnificat, anima mea, Dominus.* What a miracle! What ardor. Misericordia. Blessed are those amongst women—Blessed war! What am I saying? I blaspheme. I hope no one will come by and see me with my breast exposed. I have nothing to cover myself with; and why cover myself—the *Madonna Litta* of Leonardo Da Vinci, they are almost all with the naked breast when breastfeeding.'

"She was reborn to the world of the Madonnas, the many Madonnas she saw hanging on the walls of the convent. She was now in a state of sublime peace as the baby was sucking at her breast. Who could have imagined that that would have happened to her?

" 'Blessed are thou amongst women,' she repeated over and over.

"She looked at her breast again with satisfaction now, the *pudore* of all those years spent in the convent vanished like the morning dew kissed by the ardent rays of the July morning sun. It was enough to look at that little face, no longer tormented by hunger, to throw her into ecstasy, and she began to shout to all creation, the river, the sun, and the birds who were fluttering around her like the angels around the stable at Bethlehem.

" 'I want to be a mother; to sing thousands of lullabies to my babies. I have no shame.'

"She needed to look at that angelic face again to feel blessed among women. A sweet warmth flushed her face; an intense love was awakened within as that colostrum continued to trickle down slowly but steadily from her being into that arid little body, another being not born from her but who had become hers in that moment."

Suor Pie Marie looked down at her breast. Then got up from her sitting position on the stairs leading to the monastery, still in ecstasy, singing a melodious pianissimo. "*Benedetta fra le donne*" (Blessed are thou amongst women). She stretched her arms toward me and gently but determinedly handed me that little satisfied creature.

"Take her, she is yours! You have searched for her for a long time."

It was the first time I had heard this sad story. A spear pierced my heart, but only for an instant, for the figure of that desperate woman came to me; that woman who was my mother, who, devastated and exhausted by the birth *non grato*, abandoned herself to her pain, to her defeat as a woman, as a mother, as a wife. That snow-white figure, Suor Pie Marie, who appeared to the little group nestled under the bridge near the river in the darkness of the night, was my sweet, heroic Aunt Maria, who freed me from death's grip and gave me the language of the angels, French. To narrate is truly to remember, to return to the garden of my childhood with Aunt Maria, my Virgil, my infallible and indomitable guide. We fell into a delectable embrace and tearful eyes guided us toward the monastery in perfect silence. I, weighed down by my sad story, she, lighter to have freed herself from those lugubrious memories—to have once more called forth those memories, which had been buried in her unconscious soul, and let them come to the light of my memory so that time would not tarnish or annihilate them.

"Do you see that little road to the right of the monastery? A year later [1943], the war still raging, in a blessed moment of silence, we ventured out of the *rifugio* [shelter], sure that the German soldiers, who were stationed near the monastery for a couple of days, had left. I held you in my arms, but you, like a bird ready to fly away, struggled to free yourself from my arms and explore the ground. I put you down and you hesitantly but willingly took the first step, then another and another. My heart burst with joy. The joy of a mother."

My legs ran toward that moment, that first step. I needed only those words, "the first step," to launch me into my childhood journey, a journey very much desired but never realized till today. Why? No one spoke of it. Were they ashamed that among them lived a murderer, my Nonno? Or was it the fear of finding something painful, unacceptable, unreconcilable? Yet it was that childhood that modeled me, formed me, however travailed it was, into what I am today. It was easy to stay away from my childhood memories while I was searching for clues, for stories of my identity, but once at the monastery, that blessed ground, that staircase that led me to the heaven of truth and the thought that I would leave this blessed region in a couple of days, perhaps never to come back to again, launched me to fly on that little road that led to many other roads, bigger, narrower, scarier…

5

The Forbidden Journey

My mind was ready to cross the threshold of my memories, that forbidden world, to discover, relive, and accept the verdict, however painful it might be.

Here I was on the little country road on my weak legs, ready to show the world that, notwithstanding my malnourished body, I was alive and well, ready to embark on the greatest voyage of my life. There was so much to learn before I could venture toward the Atlantic and beyond. I fell, I got up, a game of strength, of will, to discover why I was born on that dark night of July 1942, and not in the light of the sun like many other children… why baby girls do not bring forth a smile when they come into the world. Why, *perche?* One of the first words that came out of my skeletal body. "Perche?" The most constant word on the lips of people swallowed by the monster of the Second World War. The wet nurse was never constant, only the war was. How many wet nurses I had.

"*Signora*, will you please let my baby sister suck at your breast? She is very hungry and mother is very ill," would ask my eight-year-old sister Nina as she took me around the village like the priest carried the sacred Blessed Sacrament to the sick. I, too, was sick, sick with hunger.

"Sorry, but I do not have enough milk for my child, I worked too hard in the fields today and had little to eat. *Senza cibo, no latte, anche le mucche lo sanno…*" (Without food, no milk, even the cows know it.)

And the search, the Via Crucis, continued. Now and then a woman would say yes, and my sister would throw me in her tired and sweaty arms. She would unbutton the black shirt of a widow, and put her baby on a blanket on the dirt floor, it, too, worn out by time and misery. With a sad but sweet face capable of even softening the stones, she would fix her black eyes on mine, and after such a brief exchange, I would be at her breast, from which dripped that sweet nectar of love into my inert, almost lifeless body; a body inert from hours of crying. Then she would take her baby from the floor with one hand and bring him to her other breast, and like two hungry cubs we sucked away. She was like the she-wolf that fed the twins Romulus and Remus, the founders of the city of Rome. She did not keep me at her breast for long; there were too many other mouths to feed.

The journey continued, every day the same story, until we reached Annina's house, the mother of five boys who greatly disappointed her at each birth, for she wanted a little girl as badly as my mother wanted a boy. I did not understand that crazy world. No one was happy, including my poor Nina, whose arms were aching from carrying me around. Her arms were my baby carriage. Exuberant, Annina would hold me in her powerful arms. She was well developed and well endowed, would fill my minuscule face with kisses, and joyfully put me to her breast. I was always ready to eat and would begin my task of filling myself to the brim. Annina needed no bribes; she did not need our oil and kindly offered my sister biscotti, a treat at the time, when all the food went to feed the soldiers who were dying like flies at the front. Yes, she had milk; it flowed abundantly from her generous and well-nourished body like the river in front of Marianna's house.

Oh! That blessed river. The river became for me a symbol of life, of abundance, of constancy; a place of peace, free from cares, a place to dream. The river that sang its eternal song of oblivion was my chosen, secret companion. How many lessons I learned from its perpetual song. The war was in her song; Lina's death was in her song, together with the desperate cries of the mother, echo of the anguish of every mother.

Naked like the frogs, my cousins and I would sit on the white boulders of the river and watch the water stream downward, toward the greater sea, where it would commingle with greatness and transform itself to salty water. Yes, it would lose its sweetness. But, Oh! to become part of the greater sea, to lose itself into those waves which kissed the shore, was for me an immolation and a transformation to be wished for. How fascinating my river was. It was beaming with life; eels sliding in and out, gentle waves caressing the graceful flowers adorning its banks, tadpoles in a state of flux, and above all, the children coming to talk to it as if it were a father confessor. How I loved its continuous carefree babbling that cradled my thoughts, made me forget the airplanes rumbling above us, kept my secrets and then carried them away on its waters. Where? That I did not know, I could only imagine.

That mystical river, the first teacher of my young, fragile but resilient life, invited me to dream of a better world, a world where children played outside without fear of being blown to pieces by bombs left behind by the Germans, or the American helicopters spraying DDT over all of us playing joyfully outside. A day later another helicopter sprayed us with multicolored sheets of papers announcing in Italian to keep the children in for they were going to spray for lice. Unfortunately for all of us, the announcement was too late. But I continued to be transported by the river to another world, where children did not cry because their stomachs were growling like the planes flying overhead. I dreamed of being Ulysses and visiting the island of the Sirens, the many Circes, and braving the monsters, Scylla and Charybdis. But a different

Scylla, the universal monster of death, did engulf me and brought me to the discovery of another reality.

6

My First Brush with Death

Front row (left to right): Teresa, Marianna, Antonietta, Aunt Lisa with Mary on her lap, sister Gina. Back row (left to right): Luigi, sisters Ottavia and Pina, Emma, sister Nina holding baby Lina. Arridavota, circa 1949

Marianna and I, inseparable companions, seated on the marble stones of the river, were intent in lullabying the small frog who was desperately pretending to sleep to then escape at the first opportunity from our malefic hands. But suddenly, a deafening, shrill, desperate sound drowned our lullaby and energized our little frog, who jumped into the water, free at last. Marianna and I ran as fast as our little legs could carry us toward that sound. The grief-stricken face of Aunt Lisa met our eyes. We froze in our tracks, naked to the whole world, and stared at that heartbroken, terrified mother, desperately trying to revive that defenseless wisp of flesh already rigid and pale, her infant Lina.

My mother arrived, and like a bolt of lightning, swiftly but gently removed that lifeless body from the tight grip of Aunt Lisa and, without hesitation, began to wash her with warm water and dress her in her white baptismal dress. I asked my mother why Lina needed to be washed, as she was already dead. After a quick slap on my face for asking such a foolish question, she told me that Lina was meeting our Lord, and she could not be dirty. It seemed to make sense, but I was still confused as to why my question was foolish. It seemed to me that every question I asked evoked those slaps, which hurt for a moment but lasted a lifetime.

Nevertheless, I was most curious about the whole process of washing and dressing Lina and my mother's facial expressions. I began to look intently at my mother, who had a gentle touch, sweet and maternal, as if she were afraid of hurting her. First, she closed Lina's olive black eyes, closed forever to the world of the frogs, and to her mother's smile. With loving hands, my mother deposited Lina in her crib and immediately ordered us to go to the fields and gather little white flowers to make a crown for her little head, which was becoming more and more marmoreal.

Marianna and I flew outside to announce to the river and to the fields that we needed their flowers, and we respectfully bent down to gather them ever so gently as to not disturb the bees, the butterflies and the lizards, all slumberous. Maybe they were sad too at the news and found refuge in sleep. They, too, were waiting for Lina to play with them, running after them. The river was certainly mourning Lina's death, and was heard in its lugubrious song accompanied by the sound of the bells that rang *a martorio*, the minor chords. All knew about our sudden loss, all creatures—we were all one, all connected in my little village. We all depended on one another, even on the bees, especially the bees, to pollinate our fields and fruit trees.

Marianna and I ran toward the house howling and jumping, careful not to drop the flowers; a wasp, also hungry, bit our derrières (behinds), which were exposed to the elements. We had left our underwear on a stone in the river when we heard Aunt Lisa's howl. My mother, all gentleness and loveliness toward Lina, lifted her hand and spanked us on the already painful derrieres. Like the wind we flew to the river, sat in its cool refreshing waters, which were a balm to our pain. We looked at each other and burst into a powerful laughter. We soon remembered our Lina, and Marianna began to cry. We could cry on demand like the women dressed in black at the funeral processions. However, for a few minutes I remained tearlessly contemplating my mother's reaction to our pain. Instead of soothing us with a caress, she caused more pain. I began to detest adults; I did not understand them, especially my mother, whose kindness toward others intrigued me, yet who was distant toward me. Maybe one had to be dead to evoke a mother's love.

We came back to the house in time to place the crown of wildflowers on Lina's head. We put on the white dresses of the *verginelle* (the little virgins), and like two lampposts, we stood on each side of Lina's casket, it too made by the ingenious hands of Nonno Luigi. We watched *la filastrocca* (the line) of the women of the village, all dressed in black like crows, pass before the casket, intoning a lugubrious miserere. But why such a string of sad words? The ladies did not cry, not even Lina's mother. She was seated near Lina, also marmoreal, staring at the ashen white skin. The cantilena continued; no rest, no one ran out of breath, repeating the same words over and over again:

"You will now be an angel in heaven looking down on

your mamma. Poor mamma without her Lina..."

And everyone burst into tears, real tears, perhaps, but to me the whole thing seemed theatrical, a mise en scène della Commedia dell'Arte. Everyone was transformed into thousands of Arlecchino e Columbine, their faces covered with shining colors. And I enjoyed that spectacle, thinking how little it took to create that scene. My imagination went wild. It seemed to me that all cried on demand, waiting patiently for their cue. It was necessary to be given the permission to cry, to abandon oneself to the sorrow evoked by the words: *Povera mamma senza la sua Lina...* (Poor mother without her Lina.) Adults seemed stranger than ever to me.

I stayed there on my perch, motionless, singing my own cantilena to my doleful soul, the cantilena of Suor Angelica from the opera of the same name, by Giacomo Puccini, sung to us by Mastro Antonio, on a wintery night in front of the brazier full of shining red coals, like one of the red sunsets on the Ionian coast. The brazier gave us a pleasant warmth, which climbed up our legs, leaving our derrieres cold. By the end of the opera, the front part of our legs were red and marble like the *soppressate* (salami) hanging from the fireplace chimney, which like a promontory, dominated the kitchen and surroundings, swallowing the sparks that climbed and disappeared up the chimney. I could not help but recite one stanza of the poem:

O monachine, scintillanti e belle,
Che il camino inghiotte,
Andate forse a salutar le stelle?
Buona notte faville, buona notte.
(Oh sweet little sparks that the chimney swallows,
Are you on your way to greet the stars?
Goodnight little sparks, goodnight.)

Mastro Antonio, who missed nothing, would unleash his cane on my head, calling me back from my reverie to Suor Angelica, who, kneeling in front of the altar in the convent, was singing her doleful aria to her dead baby:

Senza mamma o bimbo tu sei morto,
Le tue labbra senza i baci miei…
(Without your mother, oh child you died,
You closed your lips without my kisses…)

I, in the meantime, was asking myself (for no one was allowed to ask questions) where Mastro Antonio had learned this jewel of an opera unknown to us all; I was sure that inside Mastro Antonio there was a recording of all the operas, which was put there by an immanent force, the origin of which even he did not understand. But he was happy to be a medium sent by the Divine Providence to enlighten us and lighten the burden of war, to distract us from our hunger and the morass of a war that was grafted in everyone's heart.

"Poor mother without her Lina." Aunt Lisa, overcome by those words, like a volcano inactive for years, woke from her torpor and launched herself onto Lina's little body, emitting a desperate sound capable of waking the whole of creation, especially those doleful faces who had temporarily found peace in the repetitious cantilena. But the booming sound did not wake our Lina. I was waiting for it and waited patiently for the miracle to happen. I was waiting for that booming sound to awaken her just like it did the little frog sleeping in my hand in the river when we first heard that primordial scream. Or maybe she was going to sleep forever like all our dead. But what did I know of death?

Death was for me like everything else in nature. I would observe the flowers, first beautiful and inviting, and then they would bend their heads and be no more, only to come back again after a long vernal sleep. Then, when the bells rang announcing someone's death, I would tell myself that death was for the others and not for my family. However, Lina's death changed everything in my little head. Yes, death was real; otherwise why all that crying, those piercing sounds of Zia Lisa that shook each fiber of my body. I began to tremble like the women bitten by a tarantula, and began to dance the tarantella in my head. I imagined myself swirling around and jumping into the air at the sound of the high notes. My imagination was my gift; I could escape any sorrow, any torment, by willing myself to another place more loving, less turbulent, more receptive to my million questions.

What interested me, however, more than Lina's death, was my mother's tenderness for the little dead body. She would stroke that little face, white as a lily, and would hold her hands in hers as if she wanted to warm them up from the coldness of death. I was sure now, one had to be dead for mothers to caress their baby girls. My mother would almost never caress me. It was that day that I decided that I was not my mother's daughter but the child of a Gypsy who abandoned me on her doorstep. I tried to investigate my birth, but no one wanted to speak about it, not even the little ladies seated in a group to discuss all that had happened and was happening in the village; they would shoo me away like a fly. That silence, that brusque way, made me even more suspicious.

Lina's parents lived outside the village, in a place called Arridavota. Their house was on a hill overlooking the river, a river that served many functions. There we watched our mothers wash clothes, while we children bathed in those blessed waters, trying to catch the soap bubbles. There we emptied our bodies in the southern part of the river, and would watch the water carry the excrements away, and in their long journey they would become food for the eels which my father would catch and then cook in a delightful tomato sauce. My mother, without any suspicion from which part of the river they had come, found every morsel delicious and praised my father, the cook and the fisherman. I would laugh sotto voce, imagining that existential moment in which only a word about the *cacca* and the *pipi* we did in the river would have thrown my mother into a frantic effort to empty her stomach, just like we children emptied the sock on the sixth of January to find out what La Befana, the female version of Saint Nicholas, had brought us. Invariably, I got charcoal amid the chocolates, the oranges and the filberts, to remind me to be better behaved during the year. I, instead, took it as an insult and believed that no matter how good I was, I would get my charcoal anyway. I decided to be bad, for that's what La Befana expected. However, I would use the charcoal to draw on the paper the salt was wrapped in, a nice pale blue that went well with the black of the charcoal; I would spend hours drawing my little village. It did not take much to make me happy.

7

The Procession

The men arrived, ready to transport Lina's coffin to my house, which was in the village, a few kilometers away. We all walked in a procession. The women, all dressed in black, recited the Rosary accompanied by the sound of a recorder that emitted a melancholy sound in the still and reddish sunset sky. Some of the ladies, also dressed in black, carried on their heads braziers with live coals, which, animated by the incense, would send toward heaven an aroma so intoxicating and hypnotic that I would get lost in that smoke and fly into that infinite sky, above the clouds, and admire the procession from above: a colony of ants, a coming and going without end, procession after procession, dead people after dead people. Everything proceeded with a measured macabre rhythm. I saw Marianna and me dressed in white, jumping on the road like the eels and the frogs in the river, throwing flower petals gathered for the occasion in the air. We found delight in following those petals circle the air and then fall on Lina's coffin and on the road; others, caught by the gentle summer zephyr, flew through the air like butterflies. I adored the processions. Those ethereal petals transported me far beyond the confines of my mind, far away to the Furies, who, without any remorse, found delight in cutting the threads of my poor Lina's life and giving it to the god of death, who would change her into a soul ready to be transported by Charon's boat to the land of Hades and his wife Persephone. Hades ruled the underworld with great liberalism though, allowing Persephone to live on earth for six months to help her mother Demeter (the goddess of agriculture) with the harvest, after she was brutally snatched from Demeter's bosom by Hades himself. Hades did not have a heart of stone; he was moved by a mother's tears enough to let Persephone visit earth. Perhaps he would also be moved by Aunt Lisa's tears and let her little Lina visit her during harvest. I was full of hope. Hope was my saving grace.

Little did I know then that I, too, like Lina would be waiting for a boat one day that would take me away from the Mediterranean shores, far away from my beloved world to a new one, where every vocal sound was foreign to me, and mine to others; a macabre and unknown future where I would have to reinvent and recreate a new persona. Would I have the strength to do it, the patience to remain in front of a candle and learn to pronounce the

"TH," which in a perfect execution would have made a flame tremble? Candles were a cardinal point in my life, both during my birth and in the new world. I knew I had to succeed. I wasn't born under a bridge and didn't survive that horrible night only to give up at the sound of a "TH." An arcane force was surfacing from the womb of the earth, from its clay which had modeled me into a resilient and strong girl. Besides, I had the advantage of my age; I was young, only seventeen.

Once we arrived at my house, the procession of the ants stopped, and I descended from the clouds to the smell of coffee, taralli and the perfume of incense; the perfume of fragrant wood, which would climb toward that pink sky that was the sunset, the sunset of Lina and, I realized for the first time, the sunset of all us mortals.

The men deposited the small casket on our dining room table, which, like everything else in the village, had many functions. Lina was only a year old, but the house soon swarmed with people who rushed out of their houses at the sound of the bells. That old sing-song (cantilena) emitted by the cavernous mouths of the old ladies never seemed to end, not even with the smell of the coffee. But why those *cantilene* without end? I soon realized that that monotonous and lugubrious cantilena would fill our souls with peace and allow the tears to stream down like the water of the fountain.

The effect was obvious even to a little girl five years

old like me. The screams would cease, and the cantilena would make all present marmoreal like Lina's body. Marianna would glance at me with smiling eyes, licking her lips. Then she would return to her sad look. We were waiting for the other *verginelle* (the girls dressed in their first communion dresses) to arrive and take our place near Lina so that we would have time to sneak furtively to the kitchen before everything was devoured by the women of the *cantilene* and the family. I loved being a child, spending the days running after butterflies and capturing the frogs on the riverbanks, and the processions. Besides, I did not have to go to school. There were no schools to go to; the war had taken care of that. No television to watch, no books to read, only old ladies and men telling us stories about Hades and a myriad of other lugubrious tales about our village and its people, but no one spoke of my story, my birth under the bridge. Perhaps my story was not lugubrious enough. Most people loved to recount the Greek legends, and soon enough they were on every tongue, the story of Ulysses, of little Telemachus, his son, and his beloved wife, Penelope, who would weave her father-in-law's shroud by day and undo it by night to keep the suiters who wanted to marry her at bay. How I loved those learned teachers who taught us by telling one marvelous story after another. The whole town, children and elderly, listened intently. I was in Paradise; my imagination grew like the flowers of the valley, free to spin tales of my own, unimpeded by rules and monotonous learning. Nature in all its glory and power was my teacher, with its rivers murmuring songs of joy and sorrow, its mountains sheltering me from the voracious winds. However, now at this moment I wished to be older, but there was nothing I could do; I was still a child no matter how hard I tried to stretch my legs and stand on my toes, trying to reach those perfumed taralli (pastries in the form of donuts). I was a child; it was obvious to everyone; I didn't even have a bra. Another piercing sound escaped from the dining room...

8

Back to Serra San Bruno

That sound immediately brought me back to the present, to my Zia Maria taking her *pisolino* (siesta) under the *abeti* (fir trees) of Serra San Bruno. She woke from her *pisolino*, I from my journey of my childhood, with the perfume of that coffee still in my nostrils. I took her hand lovingly and covered it with kisses. I wanted that moment to last forever, just the two of us alone under the majestic *abeti*. I was never tired of looking at that Leonardian face, my Zia Maria, my savior. How could I leave her for a land totally alien to me? Language ceased to be relevant; it could not express my anguish. Only silence. We abandoned ourselves to that silence, to that moment so sublime when heaven and earth exist in an eternal embrace, our embrace. All else vanished.

After a while we got up slowly; she, refreshed from her *pisolino*, I, down from my clouds, and went toward the monastery. We visited San Bruno's cell, and Zia Maria began to tell me another story, that of San Bruno, the monk who left his comfortable abode in France for an unknown land dense with majestic fir trees which later took his name, Serra San Bruno. I listened but I was not present; I had no desire to listen to another story, no matter how similar it was to mine. I was immersed in my own. I kept that little body close to my heart, that hungry little girl that my aunt had given to me, and I wanted to nourish her. Yes, I did have breasts, but they were too small, the breasts of an adolescent, two buds still closed to the sun of maternity. Zia Maria, like the whales that have to come up from the deep waters to breathe, breathed out story after story and then descended to her deep sea for more. She continued to tell me many more, but I no longer had ears to hear them or the will to assimilate them into my being. Lovingly, I took her hand and brought it to her lips as a sign to stop.

How long I had been waiting to reclaim her, my little infant; seventeen years of searching and inquiries, story after story woven by my fertile imagination, and now a few days before my departure she came to me as easily as a summer breeze. I wanted now more than ever to savor this gift, follow her steps, her journey in a world bombed by foreign planes, a world where stomachs grumbled louder than the planes. But also a world full of little pleasures, and pleasant things: the ginestra (a forsythia-like plant with divinely smelling yellow flowers) that continued to fill our nostrils with the most perfumed scent and our eyes with a vision of a yellow heaven as she covered the hills and undulated with the wind; the acacia whose white blossoms, cascading from its branches not unlike grapes from their vines, called our consciousness to purity among bombs that exploded and soldiers who marched by imperiously, making the soil tremble under their feet. I must enjoy the present, my Suor Angelica, her stories, which will enlighten and lighten my solitude on the Vulcania, the boat that will take me to my underworld. I had found myself. I hugged my little being close to my breast and, without hesitation, walked toward the bus that would take us back to Capistrano.

We walked down the large stairs in silence, each absorbed in her thoughts; I was saying goodbye to the giant *abeti*, to the Certosa, uncertain that I would ever see them again. I thought of Aida, the Ethiopian princess singing goodbye to her land in the opera by the same name.

> *Oh dolci campi o profumate rive,*
> *Oh Patria mia mai più' ti rivedro'*
> *Mai più, mai più' ti rivedro'...*
> (Oh sweet fields, oh perfumed rivers,
> I will not see you again... never again.)

We sat on the bus, one near the other, holding hands, silent like two Sphinx looking at the magnificent panorama, savage, yes, but beautiful. Nature was in her prime, not yet tamed by man but left to her own devices, to grow wildly and harmoniously. I could not get enough of that mountainous and tortured countryside, which very much resembled my soul.

As we traveled toward the village, I thought: should I remain mute like the saints in the church, or confront my mother and grandfather about my findings? Or hope that the sea, once I was on the ship, would bring me oblivion like it did to Ulysses when he heard the Sirens calling him? Perhaps the sound of the waves would be my lotus flower, the sea, my island of Circe, and I would obliterate the past. Silence is golden but not redemptive. Should I bury my newly found treasure and unearth it later, once I found understanding and with it forgiveness? Not knowing what to do, I abandoned myself to sleep, that great doctor that cures body and soul. Zia Maria, too, abandoned herself to sleep, tired of having relived and told my story.

We woke at the sound of the bells announcing the Angelus, and my little village came into view, small and fragile, resting on a hill. My life shone in front of my eyes like a continuum, no longer in pieces but as a united whole; there was no longer the tormenting past, for today I was told about my birth, nor any future, because in a few days I would leave for a land unknown to me, a land that did not belong to me. Its culture, its language, its modus operandi were to me as strange as the shores were to Aeneas in his first encounter with the country he was about to found, Italy.

For me there was nothing else but the present. My life extended in the present like a long line from which, instead of clothes, hung panels on which were written my life events, each shone and hummed in the sun of my mind, and undulated at the touch of every thought. My life had neither beginning nor end—a continuum extending ad infinitum. I felt whole, living every moment as if it were my last.

9

Shall I or Shall I Not...

The bus came to a stop; my adored aunt ran home to her little ones, who were waiting for her like hungry birds in the nest. I ran toward my Nonno, who, seated as usual under the acacia tree, was reading his paper. He saw me and waved his powerful hands, signaling me to come near. He offered me his bony knees to sit on and began to tell me about his long voyage on a boat toward New York, and from there to California, in search of gold.

"Eat, eat, when you are on the boat, it is a long trip; even if you throw up, something will remain in your stomach," he told me with authority but lovingly. I hardly listened to his story about the cowboys and their wild tales. For the love of God not another story, I thought. My mind swam in stories. My eyes were fixed on his enormous hands like never before; malevolent hands that had attempted to snuff out my nascent life, a life that had not yet heard the enchanting voice of Suor Angelica, my aunt, with her arpeggios that went toward heaven like incense.

As Nonno talked, he gesticulated with his hands, the hands I had so greatly admired as a child as he created masterpieces: furniture, oil refineries, barrels to put wine in and wooden shoes for us children, just to mention a few. I could not stop watching his hands as he built my doll furniture. He spoke without stopping. I did not dare interrupt him; he was lost in the Wild West chasing wild horses... I waited patiently for a break to ask him why he did not want me to live, but no luck; the darkness engulfed us and swallowed us whole. He got up, still moving his hands in the air and disappeared into his labyrinth. Groping in the dark, I was able to find my way up the stairs to confront my mother.

My mother was seated near the fireplace with her friends, all silently sobbing. My mother's face appeared so pale and opaque in the light of the oil lamp that I felt her pain. The anguish of leaving her home, where she had lived for fifty-eight years, where she had experienced the horrors of two world wars and had seen her young mother die, heartbroken to leave her two-year-old baby in her care only to have to bury him weeks later due to scarlet fever. Taken by pity, I did not think this was the right time to hit her with my sad discovery. I wished everyone a good night, and holding my young being dearly in my arms, I went to bed.

10

Susu

"Tomorrow I will wake up early," I told myself. I wanted to once again see the sun rising on my ancient world, where life seemed immutable, where time seemed to have been stopped. Awakened by the sound of the bells announcing the beginning of another day, I heard footsteps coming from the outside. I ran to the window and saw a figure go by. An apparition, a ghost, the dead returning to their marmoreal homes. Oh yes, I had to go to the cemetery to say goodbye to my ancestors. How many things to do before I sailed away.

The figure of a woman appeared under my window. She looked up and reproached me for being awake at that ghastly hour. She invited me to go with her to the hills where she owned some property, called Susu, to gather broccoli di rape and other wild herbs.

"Come, your mother likes them," said my aunt Albina, my mother's youngest sister, who was called thus for she was born at dawn.

Albina was raised by Donna Micuccia, a childless widow, my Nonno's sister, after Albina's mother died. Donna Micuccia was respected by all the women of our village and the nearby ones for her talent at the loom, that ancient tool which took a real expert to program. She was called to do the programming by many people in the Calabria region.

When she was at home, she spent her days navigating the spool, called *navetta*, among the thousands of threads programmed in many ways to make beautiful silk, linen and cotton cloth displaying exquisite designs. Programming the loom was a difficult task, and few in our region would have the required skills.

I went down, opened the door gently not to wake my mother and, enveloped by that misty light, entered the world of my Zia Albina, who, notwithstanding the darkness, grabbed my ear and pulled it; luckily, I did not have earrings so she did not damage my ear. She loved to pull ears and laugh with such pleasure, as if her task in life was to pull ears, and to make bread in her large *madia*, a trough-like wooden object into which she would put a sack of flour, yeast and water. I was amazed to see how a woman of her small stature could manage it all. She would get the yeast from the stomach of a baby goat, a small ball full of milk that the poor beast had just sucked from the utters of his mother, who, unaware that that would be the last time, did not smell, caress or give a last kiss to her baby goat. He died without his mother, just like Suor Angelica's baby in Puccini's opera by the same name. As I imagined all those little stomachs hanging in the sun to dry, tears began to stream down my cheeks for those poor creatures. I found refuge in my musical mental labyrinth and began to sing sotto voce the following aria:

> *Senza mamma o bimbo tu sei morto*
> *Le tue labbra senza i baci miei*
> *Scoloriron fredde fredde!*
> *E chiudesti, o bimbo, gli occhi belli.*
> (Without your mother, oh my sweet child, you died, without my kisses… Your beautiful eyes, my child, grew dim and closed forever.)

Nothing was bought in our village, not even Puccini's music, which was given to us as a gift by Mastro Antonio, who knew every aria and score and would pull them out of his being as easily as a magician pulls a rabbit from his hat. From his mouth would come out authentic sounds of various instruments: the clarinet, the violin, the flute, entire orchestration pieces from the various operas. What an artist! I was convinced that Mastro Antonio was not born from a woman but came out from Orpheus's body, who, guilty of being responsible for his wife Euridice's metamorphosis into stone, came back to earth from the underworld and created Mastro Antonio as a gift to us villagers, who, devastated by war, were ready to accept such a sublime act, the gift of music, which helped us go beyond the morass of the moment. We never felt sad or hungry when we listened to music; it was as if another force entered our bodies and lifted us to something greater than our growling stomachs. The universe provided us with the necessities to nourish our souls so that we would not go mad.

Aunt Albina and I walked in silence, in prayer, as if we did not want to disturb nature's work, which was slowly manifesting itself, first, with the sound of the birds breaking the stillness of the air; secondly, with the light filtering through the trees, giving them shape as they came out of their slumberous selves. The moon, with its less brilliant silvery face, still bright enough in the sky to illuminate our way, which became steeper and steeper, slowing our pace.

I, absorbed in my thoughts, saw myself near a marvelous woman, strong, generous, altruistic, inviting the neighbors every year to make the *voti* (pastry) for the feast of San Rocco; a medieval tradition that women like her kept alive.

The *madia* (a big, long wooden bowl, a couple of meters long) once more was full to the brim with flour made from the wheat from her fields and eggs from her many hens which roamed her garden and entered her kitchen singing the cluck, cluck, announcing that they had laid the eggs—a deafening sound that challenged my more developed auditory canals.

My aunt and a consort of women continued their work preparing the dough, which later in their able hands was transformed into a multitude of limbs: feet, legs, hands, heads with all the apparatus, torso and internal organs like heart, lungs, stomachs; an anatomical array never seen in Leonardo da Vinci's laboratory.

Once the women finished modeling the *voti*, they were baked in a big stone oven heated by the branches and wood that Zia Albina brought in bundles on her head from the mountains. Once cooked, the *voti* were taken out with a long, flat wooden shovel and deposited on long, skinny wooden tables where they were decorated with a white *ingilippo* (sugar and egg white).

This process required great skill and was done with concentration, because the *voti*, apparently solid and strong like rocks, were fragile enough to break easily. Especially the heads, with eyes, ears, noses protruding out, were most vulnerable. Everything had to be perfect when presented to San Rocco, who was implored to heal the particular part of the body each *voto* represented.

Zia Albina's laboratory was one which showed no signs of progress, a mixture of chemistry and tradition immune to change and marching to an immutable ancient rhythm resurrected once a year. Everyone participated in this tradition; even the children worked diligently, beating the egg whites and the sugar in immense bowls made from the sacred limbs of the olive trees that graced the surrounding landscape with their majestic stature, emanating a heavenly smell when in bloom. The children loved this task, beating vigorously until it all became white peaks of snow, tempting them to furtively stick their tongue or finger in the bowl. God forbid one was caught, for he or she would be severely punished and disqualified for the following year's ritual.

Once the peaks of sugar reached their highest level, the able hands of the women took over. They covered the *voti* with the white mixture, making the body parts more attractive, less bellicose and more appetizing. The smell of vanilla permeated every corner of the kitchen. We children could no longer stand to wait for the feast of San Rocco, and more immediately, for the women to finish decorating the *voti* and hand us the empty bowl to let our tongues finish the work. We loved the feast of San Rocco.

Every household made the *voti*, even those who did not have any infirmities. They pretended they had some and would make the whole body to offer to the saint to protect them from the *malocchio* (the evil eye), which, like *la calunnia* (slander) in the opera *il Barbiere di Siviglia*, would spread like wildfire, first slowly, and then in a crescendo entering the auditory canal of the people, and then buzzing around, causing havoc and becoming stronger as it installed itself in the subconscious of the young and old. Everyone feared the *malocchio*.

La calunnia e' un venticello...

Slander is like a breeze which at first appears soft and gentle, but then, as it makes its rounds, becomes a hurricane, destroying reputations, at times whole families.

Like the *calunnia*, the fragrance of the *voti* came out of every kitchen, and together with the perfume of the ginestra brought down from the mountains by the gentle zephyr, would send old and young into ecstatic rapture of joy and goodness. In my village we were always in a state of transition between tears and joy. We lived "*a fior di pelle*," would say the old ladies who, no longer able to sustain the pace of everyday living, would give themselves to observation and dispensing dictums to the younger ones caught in the frenetic rhythm of daily demands. Patience! This was the way we were made, modeled from the clay that was extracted from the womb of our land.

The day of the feast, which occurred on the second Sunday of September, all the children, called *verginelle*, dressed in white with a crown of flowers on their heads representing the purity of girls, which was guarded by their parents and the whole village. Those girls whose purity was violated were not only punished severely, sometimes ending in death, but if they survived the wrath, they were isolated from the community and branded as outcasts. The perpetrators were punished by being banned temporarily from the village, only to return later and be pardoned by a society that saw women as the temptresses, the Mary

Magdalenes portrayed by the church.

I never understood as a child why women always paid the price for being abused; even in the operas that Mastro Antonio sang, the sopranos ended up dying or being sent to a convent like Suor Angelica.

To the sound of the band, all the children came out of their houses like the children in the fable "The Pied Piper of Hamelin." We all marched in a solid, measured pace, like marionettes set to motion, not by pulling strings, but by the ancient force of tradition, by the call of San Rocco of Montpelier, who left his country, France, to find refuge in this small, mountainous terrain suspended between sky and sea.

San Rocco was in the piazza waiting for everyone: women carrying on their heads large baskets full of body parts decorated in white; dogs that barked at the clay dog who stood proudly near the saint; they too, wanted to climb the wooden platform and be with San Rocco's dog and see themselves in the mirror of tradition. Don Basilio, the priest dressed in white like a huge *verginella* (little virgin), was waiting with the young boys dressed in white. Then the piazza would fill with people, and at the sound of the *tamburo*, the procession would begin. The women, especially the old ones, would begin singing, emitting from their cavernous mouths sounds rendered more haunting by the lack of teeth. These strident sounds were able to wake up all creation, the frogs slumberous under a stone, the crickets, the butterflies and the bees still immobile, waiting for the warm sun to heat their bodies and begin flying, announcing to all creatures that it was a solemn day. It was the day to celebrate this miraculous saint who would heal everyone's ailments.

Once the procession finished, during which time the people would offer San Rocco their *voti* representing their particular ailments, we would all gather in the piazza, where my father, like a god descended from Mount Olympus, feet planted on the steps of the church with San Rocco near him, would begin auctioning the *voti* at the sound of the *tamburo*.

Everyone bought according to their medical needs, convinced that San Rocco would heal them. My mother, suffering from an ulcer on the front part of her right leg, bought a leg made by herself donated to the saint to help her heal. We couldn't wait to go home and sink our teeth into that leg. We were hoping mother had more ailments than that so we would have more *voti* to devour. We were always hungry; it was, after all, postwar time. But the most magical moment for us was when the heads were auctioned. My mother, who made the *voto* in the form of her head because she always had a headache, would buy her own head. As my father pulled the *voti* out from the baskets made from the ginestra stocks, a perfume filled the air, making all of us crazy, including the wasps, who were never far away from the village, buzzing around the perfumed ginestra.

And the people would buy, and Don Basilio, happy as an Easter egg, would look joyously at the money that rang like the church bells as it hit the metal collection bowls. We children, planted near San Rocco, would lick our lips, hoping that a *voto* would fall from my father's powerful hands and break in a thousand pieces on the Romanesque piazza. But we waited in vain; those hands of a god kept everything firmly inside. Patience! We waited, hoping that our mothers would buy one of those heads. I was sure my mom would, for she had many headaches, especially in the evening when my father came home.

I would fix my eyes, however, on Zia Albina, she too licking her lips upon seeing all those ears. Finally, the prey appeared, a sweet, unsuspecting lady on whom Zia launched herself like a rapacious bird on her ear, made not from tarallo (an egg pastry), but from real flesh. The lady, caught by surprise, emitted a piercing primordial sound that caused Zia Albina to desist, but not from throwing a fierce admonitory look toward me ordering me to be quiet about what I had witnessed.

Once the auction was finished, San Rocco was brought into the church and deposited in his niche near Saint Nicholas of Bari, a bishop who rescued many poor children who were now represented near him in a container not unlike the one we made wine in, and looking desirous like us to sink their ceramic teeth into a head of a *voto*. As a child I was always wondering why San Nicholas would put children whom he supposedly loved in a container, and why our parents would tell us that if we misbehaved we would end up with San Nicholas. Another mystery enveloping me in this ancient village.

After the auction, the people would return to their homes carrying their *voti* wrapped in white embroidered linens to a sumptuous meal of fresh pasta dressed with *ragu al capretto* (goat in a tomato sauce), freshly grated parmigiano and tons of basil, the divine spice essential to any Italian dish. Then the much-awaited dessert, in our case the leg and the head (*voti*), fixing our eyes on our mother to see signs of the miracle. Content and full, we would all fall into a soporific siesta, our heads full of body parts, operatic sounds and processions. Every feast finished this way, in a dream.

The sound of the bells announcing the Angelus woke me from my reverie, and the mountain house came into view. We had arrived.

Zia Albina took a rusty key out of her pocket and put it in the keyhole. The door, at that magic touch, opened its enormous mouth, and a dark, empty space invited us in. We entered and opened the little window, through which a multitude of pale sunrays entered and diminished the void. Zia immediately lit the fire and fell asleep, seated in front of that balsamic heat, while I remained alone, awake, nervous and afraid, ready to receive every sound. I heard wolves in the distance howling to the moon as if it were falling onto them. Boars, like the rhinoceros in the Pirandellian comedy *The Rhinoceros*, marched through the countryside, destroying everything in sight and, reaching our temporary shelter, emitting a ghastly sound that caused my hair to stand straight on my head. I wanted to wake Zia, who remained always impervious to crisis, but decided instead to remain in front of the window, trembling like a reed, watching the spectacle.

Trying desperately to focus my thoughts on something other than that horrendous coming and going of wild boars, who seemed to find delight in running and bumping into one another, I saw a basket near the chimney. It was covered with a big linen napkin as white as the sand of the desert. I looked into it and saw a dish of peppers and potatoes (called *pipi e patati* in dialect) fried to perfection. My eyes opened as wide as the window, and I was tempted to taste them, but my mind recalled another event, where the dish of *pipi e patate* was everyone's favorite.

It was late August when the wheat would be gathered and then put through a big machine that separated the wheat from the chaff. It was a glorious day. We the children, called Persephones, would help gather the wheat stalks left behind by the big machine into bundles. We put the bundles of wheat into big containers made by the matriarchs of the village, who would sit under the acacia trees, working and talking about the birth of their babies, the pain involved, their joy when it was a boy and the sadness when it was a girl. On many of these occasions, I would patiently sit there hoping that they would talk about my birth, but none would say a word. It was the silence of the tomb which I encountered every time I asked how and when I was born.

The fields were festive; everyone sang favorite songs like "Quel mazzolin di fiori che vien dalla montagna..." (That bouquet of flowers that comes from the mountains...) The air vibrated with sounds of the machines, of the workers screaming orders right and left... a cacophony of sounds that, like incense, climbed toward heaven to disturb the celestial peace. The birds flew over our heads making strident sounds. Fortunately, our voluminous hair was wrapped by a kerchief as protection from the black birds, who, driven by hunger, would fly close to our heads over the freshly threshed fields, not unlike the birds in the painting by Vincent Van Gogh, *Wheatfield with Crows*.

At noon the bells rang in the town, announcing that it was time for a break, and everyone stopped working, silencing the threshing machine, and sat down to an abundant meal. The men would first wash their hands in the rivulet nearby and then sit on the soft grass to nourish and rest their bodies. Zia Albina always prepared her favorite dishes: *pipi e patate*, stuffed peppers, eggplants, zucchini, and my favorite, fried zucchini flowers, which were first dipped in batter and then deep fried. To accompany the fresh ricotta and salami of every kind was the delicious crusty bread made in the big wooden *madia* the day before. The local wine made by Uncle Francesco was served abundantly.

The scene was idyllic. Absent was my grandmother Dirce, who, dressed in white, often in the suffocating heat of midday, would go to the fields to visit the workers and read to them from *The Divine Comedy*, a very difficult book written in verses. I would accompany her often, for I loved her Lombardian accent, and during one of these excursions I dared to ask why she would read a book so difficult for people who knew neither how to read nor write. Even erudite people would have difficulty with *The Divine Comedy*, the most complex dream ever dreamed. She stopped walking, took my hands into hers and said sweetly: "I don't expect them to understand; I read poetry to calm their tired spirit so that refreshed, they soar above their daily burdens."

After eating, the workers, a little inebriated by the *vino locale*, returned to their labor. Everything was in movement once again. The threshing machine, with its steady beat, began to devour the bunch of wheat without ever showing signs of being full. I loved to watch the grains of wheat roll out of that vortex, shining under *il sol leone* (the lion sun) like diamonds breaking the light into millions of colors. The wheat then tumbled into sacks which, once full and securely tied, were put on the cart pulled by two donkeys, headed for the mill, where the precious grains became flour, mostly to feed Zia's family. Some of the black birds circled and circled around our heads so much so that they lost *la bussola*, their sense of direction, and fell on the heads of the unfortunate girls, losing themselves in their capillary labyrinth; we all had thick, black velvety hair.

Zia, awakened by the deafening grunting of the boars, not yet exhausted by running one after the other, began to laugh hysterically at me standing in terror, straight like a cane near the window. I covered my ears so that she would not grab them and looked at her with surprise and admiration, for this woman was afraid of nothing, even the dark. She faced each situation with Herculean force and loud infectious laughter. Immediately, she pulled out the basket, and we began to have a copious breakfast of *caffe* and goat milk, salami, cheeses and her delicious crusty bread. The noise of the boars dissipated with the light of the morning, a faint sun still warm and pleasing. Nature was awake, the birds circled the vast sky, the bees began buzzing, the wildflowers opened their eyes to a new day; everything was moving in the visible and invisible universe, and God, pleased with His handiwork, smiled over us. As always, charcoal in hand, I began to write on the white plastered walls of the little house.

> *Pennellate di Colori*
> *Filtrati dal Sole*
> *Un'immagine di Tenerezza*
> *Di Bellezza*
> *Dio.*
> (Brush strokes of colors
> Light filtering through
> An image of Tenderness
> And Beauty
> God.)

Satisfied and pleased to have eaten so much, we went out to face the elements, she holding me by my hand to cross through the line of boars, who stood there as if in a meeting. We filled our sacks with rapini and left for the village before the sun beat on our heads, already warmed by the weight of the rapini. The descent, even when loaded like mules, seemed easier. We arrived home at the sound of the bells that joyfully announced the celebration of the daily Mass.

11

My Last Day in Capistrano

Only a day was left for me to enjoy this blessed village protected by the ever-vigilant Madonna; then the trip to Napoli where Vulcania, the old white ship, was waiting in the port to take us to a land far, far away, where a cornucopia of new sounds signified nothing was waiting for us. Yet, I was excited to meet my father, and my sisters, Nina, Gina and Pina, who had delivered a healthy boy called Pino. I was finally an aunt and could not wait to hold him in my arms. But the question buzzed in my mind: What kind of aunt would I be? Would I be as exemplar as my beloved Aunt Maria, who to this day reigns supreme in my heart? But to leave my Capistrano would cause excruciating pain to me and my mother. We were both used to living with only each other, and it would be difficult for both of us to enter into the exigences of a family. Families are a great gift but also a great burden.

Aware now more than ever that time flies, I ran out of

MY LAST DAY IN CAPISTRANO

the house and toward the church situated at the center of the village in a little but graceful piazza. I entered the church to greet the Madonna della Montagna, who, seated in her niche above the major altar at the center of the church, was there, forever vigilant of her little town and its inhabitants. The Madonna looked happy in her little, mountainous village and wanted to remain there forever.

Aunt Beth, a little eighty-year-old, seemingly absorbed in prayer, saw me, and came to sit in the pew beside me. Without hesitation she began to tell me the story of our Madonna, admonishing me never to forget her. She took my hand and began to tell me the whole story as if I had never heard it before. I listened politely and occasionally I nodded yes to her demands to send money to the Madonna, and she would pin them to her dress when she passed in front of my house during the procession. Remember when you and the other children, dressed like little virgins all in white, spread fresh flower petals in front of the Madonna? The best linens and silks, embroidered by your mother, hang from your balcony. I can see them now, undulating by the breeze, which gave them life in multicolored waves. I was amazed how many details she remembered. I wished my memory would be as sharp as hers when I reached old age.

She continued on, telling me that in the last few years it had become difficult to finish the procession for old people like her, for Capistrano was full of little ascending and descending roads, a village for the young, and yet the young were all going to America, leaving the old ones to their memories. I tried to console her by telling her that I also found it an arduous procession, and one needed deep devotion to reach the finishing line, walking and singing loudly above the sound of the brass, which blasted its notes in the limpid, sweltering air with mighty force. She stressed how much she loved the "Triumphal March" from the opera *Aida* by Verdi, which completed the procession. I asked how she knew that it was Verdi's "Triumphal March," and amazed at my question, she informed me that everyone knew it. Mastro Antonio would go to the piazza and often sing opera. She smiled with pleasure.

She continued, saying that after the procession, the Madonna was brought back to the church and placed on a table covered with a tablecloth made of silk and embroidered by my beautiful sisters. Each flower that was on that tablecloth to honor our Madonna was grown in our fields.

The villagers, happy again to have fulfilled their duty, returned to their homes to food and wine. Inebriated, the men fell asleep, leaving us women to clean and be ready to serve them coffee when they woke up. "Being a woman is not easy, remember that. That's why your poor mother, tired of having girls, seven with you, cried at your birth." Another detail that I was not aware of. She continued

MY LAST DAY IN CAPISTRANO

singing the praises of our Madonna, who according to her was very rich because of the many golden rings on her fingers and jewels on her crown.

Zia Beth was showing signs of tiredness, but she felt obliged to tell me the whole story as if I were hearing it for the first time. She admonished me not to trust foreigners, for they were always after their own interest. I listened attentively and loved hearing her speak in dialect. The foreigners, she said, were sure the Madonna would bring them a good sum. They began to lift her and bring her to the carriage pulled by two donkeys, but the Madonna became so heavy that she could not be moved. The men left without our Madonna, angry and hungry. All that sweat for nothing.

I loved this story so much that every time I visited the church, it surfaced in my brain and I was never tired of hearing it. I accompanied Zia Beth home, gave her a huge hug, holding her frail body in my arms for the last time.

As a child, I was fascinated by our Madonna and would go to pray to her, telling her all my childish diatribes, one of which was why I was not beautiful like her and had black hair like the night. I also would ask her why she was blond in a village of black heads. Everything in my village seemed a mystery to me.

I heard my father telling us the story of the Madonna for the first time when I was five years old. I found comfort that, in my ugliness, no one would kidnap me.

Everyone spoke of my ugliness in the village, telling the story over and over that I was so ugly when I was born that my parents had difficulty finding people to accept to be my godparents. Finally, Uncle Ottavio and my Zia Maria accepted the task out of love, and so I was baptized in the church of the Madonna della Montagna. No liqueurs or pink confetti were offered to the few people who came to our house after the ceremony. It was wartime and food was scarce. There was nothing available to buy; all the food went to feed the soldiers. Our money had no value and was used by us children as toilet paper.

Aunt Maria and Aunt Albina brought a few dried figs and some taralli to my gathering, people say. My father disappeared from this non-festive, lugubrious scene, without a doubt going to console himself with a glass of wine at the bar nearby and remaining in that smoky atmosphere till the wee hours of the morning. The bar was purposely kept cumulous so the people could not see that the wine they were consuming was half water.

I was five years old when it dawned on me that it was my fault my father drank. Had I been a boy, I would have gone hunting with him and perhaps he would not have been in this miserable condition. I thought of telling my sisters about my guilt feelings, but I knew they would not understand. I told Peppina, the disabled girl in the town who loved us Renda children and even dared to beat up anyone who made fun of my skeletal body. But Peppina was in her own world most of the time and had no ears to listen to my stories. But we all loved Peppina, and she visited every house of the village, telling over and over the story of how my father brought her home from the insane asylum. She was not insane; she had mental disabilities, and all of us children loved her and included her in our games: the redemption of living in a small community where everyone was his brother's keeper.

Even though my father was not at the baptismal ceremony, he always spoke highly of me. "My Teresina is the most intelligent child in Capistrano," he would say with such pride and so often that I could not believe he wanted me to be a boy. I loved my father. He was the benefactor of the village: everyone's helper; the Sunday butcher who was helped by my sister Nina and distributed the newly killed goat to every woman who came in front of our house. For those who had no money to pay, he would tell my Nina to write their names in the red book. "Do not worry, my dear friend, take the meat, you will pay me when you can." Everyone knew, my father included, that they would not be able to pay, but the comedy continued until the last ounce of meat was distributed, bones and all. My father seemed to me to be the god of abundance and generosity.

We girls had a deep love for our parents, regardless of their behavior, which seemed strange at times. I think I loved them the most, I, the least wanted. As the years went by, I understood how forgiving children are; their mission is to love and to forgive everything and everyone, even the most malevolent parent. They forgive, not because they are not conscious of the parents' actions and the suffering that such actions often inflict, but for the fact that built within the children is the need to love their parents and to be loved by them in return.

I left the house and went toward the cemetery to say *addio* (goodbye) to my ancestors. The cemetery was enveloped in a mantle of peace. The dead had already reentered their tombs after a night of wandering, and were patiently waiting for night again to resume their excursions. So thought Great-Grandmother Maria. I visited her grave and became aware of time, which marches at its own pace. All of us, living and dead, follow that march, now joyfully, now funereally, but always moving between life and death, the two cardinal points that frame our existence. I felt connected to the dead members of my family and to everything in the universe big or small, alive or dead. I saw myself as a tree, a stone, a river flowing, singing the eternal song of love, of togetherness, of being. If we all felt this interconnectedness, we would become people of peace rather than war.

I stopped in front of the tomb of the Renda family. The photographs of Dirce and Giuseppe, my paternal grandparents, made me think of their story of a love so strong that Dirce had forsaken her parents in Brazil to settle in a mountainous village at the end of the Italian boot. Theirs was a love tested by prejudice, of North against South, of two cultures that do not mix, just like water and oil. Their story touched me deeply, and I wanted to remain there with them to write it, but I decided that I had thirteen days surrounded by sky and water, and all the time needed to write about my ancestors, who, pilgrims of the world, would understand my pain, my pain of leaving my beloved Capistrano.

I continued my walk and reached the tomb of the Pasceri: Grandmother Marianna, Uncle Carlo and Great-Grandmother Maria. Carlo was conscripted into the Italian regiment i Bersaglieri, so called because they carried a big hat on their heads decorated with colored feathers that moved gracefully with the least movement of the head. When Carlo came back from the front in the First World War for R&R, the children greeted him with exuberance and admiration, all vowing to become Bersaglieri when they grew up. My mother was one of these children, and often told us the story that Carlo put her on his knees and told her that this was the last time he would see her. He gave her a big kiss, and they all went to the table to eat. This wonderful dinner was to be their last supper; the war was going badly, and Carlo had no illusion of coming back alive.

The story of Great-Grandmother, called Donna Maria, surfaced to my mind. She was Carlo's mother. According to the legend, Maria would go out at night toward the piazza, would greet the Madonna by looking through the keyhole of the church and then, by the light of an oil lantern, would reach the cemetery. Once there, she would stop at the tomb of her Carlo, who was declared dead in combat soon after his visit home, and would call him to join her. He would come out and stay with her all night, reentering the tomb at the sound of the bells announcing a new day. Donna Maria, then, would return home, happy to have spent the whole night with her beloved Bersagliero, whose picture in uniform was installed on the family tomb.

I got up solemnly and slowly, as if I did not want to interrupt that encounter between mother and son, stroked my knees, bruised from kneeling on the rough pebbles and, deeply saddened by this doleful story, proceeded toward Chiazzarello, where I was sure to find my muse, my Aunt Maria. I felt a chill in the air. Autumn was still with us; its signs were everywhere. The leaves of the chestnut trees had turned into a warm brown rendered heavy by the dew that, notwithstanding the late morning, was lingering on the creation. It was not in any hurry to leave; maybe it was like me. I also was not in any hurry to be born to this world, a world upside down; a world totally gone crazy, deaf to the songs of the birds, or to the cries of the children who were afraid of the bombs.

12

Chiazzarello

Zia Maria

Here I was at Chiazzarello, a marvelous place where nature and man coexisted in sweet harmony, working together to produce fruits of every kind: vegetables, grapes, olives and flowers, like the fragrant ginestra which adorned the fields and the immense gorge, toward which I found great pleasure unleashing my frustrations by yelling them out, only to hear their echo come back to me. It is not easy to unburden one's soul; only the confessional existed for us Catholics. What power a priest has: to forgive and send you home to sin no more. I always had to invent sins to tell the priest; I felt I would disappoint him if I had no sinful stories to tell. I was amazed how easy it was to be a Catholic, you do whatever you want and then go and confess, and your soul would again be white as snow. Everything seemed absurd and unreal in my childish mind; only the war was real. I could palpate it, feel it, see it with my own eyes, like the time we were playing in the hills surrounding the village, and one of our little friends saw something that was shiny. She bent down to pick it up, and a loud sound ensued. We all got frightened and ran away, only to realize when we reached the bottom of the hill that our little friend was not with us. We ran back and her hand was bleeding. We helped her down, and once we reached her house, all crying hysterically, her mother reprimanded us for touching shiny objects that didn't belong to us. I was thoroughly confused by the behavior of adults.

I continued on in that enchanted place, where gorges echoed my thoughts and everything spoke of the love and care my Zia Maria gave to every living being. I would miss it greatly. Maybe I would have to rely on my memory to recreate this lost paradise; thank God I had a strong one, ready to recall every experience of my young life.

I opened the gate and followed the sonorous notes of sacred hymns which ascended the heavens like incense. Zia Maria was praying, "Ora et Labora," the motto of the Benedictines. I stopped and, very much moved by that sonorous sound, knelt down and sang the "Ave Maria" that Desdemona sang to the Madonna before Otello killed her in a fit of jealousy. I thought of all the wrong perpetrated on women by their men, brothers, fathers... men of the village. Maybe this was one of the reasons why my mother did not want girls and welcomed me with pain at my birth.

Immediately, the image of Vicenza came in front of me, a sweet woman with a face full of marks which spoke of her suffering. Every night after sunset she would knock at our door and, with an urgent voice, ask to be let in. She would tell us, crying desperately, that her husband would beat her every night without provocation. She wanted to know how to remedy the situation. My mother would give her the usual hug and dry her tears. One night, Vicenza appeared, howling from pain, showing us a swollen eye, black and blue. She looked like a monster. My father happened to be home and, seeing poor Vicenza in desperate condition, grabbed her by the arm and both went to Vicenza's house. With a violent kick, he opened the door and they found Nicola, the husband, drunk on the floor.

My father grabbed him by the neck and slapped him numerous times till the beast had no more voice to yell. My father let go of Nicola and sternly told him: "Women are loved, not beaten," and left the house like a bolt of lightning. Nicola never abused his wife again. I understood then why women wanted sons who would defend them from predators.

I stopped remembering and followed that sweet sound which brought me to my Zia Maria, who was bent over, trimming the grapevines which, in spring, would wake from their slumber, covering their naked stems with leaves and flowers, which would then transform into a bunch of grapes. Everything in nature was in a state of metamorphosis. I felt a part of nature; my new metamorphosis would begin with the ship leaving my sacred shores. Zia Maria saw me and welcomed me with open arms. We fell into an embrace, tears streaming down our faces. We sat near the apparently inert vines and began our sumptuous breakfast of fresh ricotta, homemade bread and olives, accompanied by *latte e caffe*. We sat in silence, as if in meditation. Finally, she broke the silence and said: "I knew you would come. I wanted to invite you, but you have many people to say goodbye to and little time left before your departure." Again, we abandoned ourselves to eating the ricotta, which was still warm and delicious. This was our last breakfast at Chiazzarello, the two of us alone in that blessed place, where nature and man coexisted in harmony and peace under the immensity of a clear sky.

Looking at the vineyard, my mind full of memories, I began to recall some of the most joyous moments in my life, when under a warm blue autumnal sky we would come to Chiazzarello to turn the ripened bunch of grapes into wine. My father had built a cement cistern for the occasion. Everyone participated, even Nonno Luigi, who was in his customary role of serious and dictatorial patriarch most of the time. But he was able, during this sacred rite, to let out a smile from his cavernous, toothless mouth. In no time he, too, was enveloped by the joyfulness of the festival.

We, the children five years and older, would be immersed in a portable bathtub made of copper, for cleaning the body. My sister Nina, the oldest, found great pleasure in soaping us head to toe with the soap she and my mother had made from the last pressing of the olives. We would wear panties and old cotton shirts that mother had woven on the loom. We climbed the wooden stairs and jumped into the cistern, full of newly picked grapes. Everything was orchestrated by Nonno Luigi, who was ingenious in designing every tool needed for the *vendemmia* (the harvesting). He was a great builder but had little patience with us children. I remembered many episodes when we, the grandchildren, would descend upon him, and he would chase us away, imploring us to stop, and when we continued our loud games, he would yell out: "Stop if you can, if not, continue." We, deaf to his decrees, would continue to play and lick our lips as we watched him chew with his gums the biscotti he had bought from the merchant who would visit the village once a week. We children were always hungry and, not able to satisfy our hunger, would surrender to our games of running uncontrollably and to the deafening sounds of the wooden sandals that grandfather had made for us all from the leftover pieces of wood he used to make furniture.

Once in the cistern, we jumped up and down on the grapes till they became a soft *poltiglia* (mash), not unlike liquid marmalade. Then the mash would be put into sacks and carried to the press nearby, where the wine juice would come out through a spigot into gigantic jugs. We, exhausted from all the jumping, lay on the ground and watched with amazement till the last drop dripped out. Then the jugs were closed and ready to be loaded onto two donkeys at sunset for the transport home.

How generous nature was! The vines gave their fruit freely and generously, without assessing who deserved it or not. There was so much to learn from nature, and I, great observer, noticed and kept everything in my little head. Uncle Carmelo, passionate about music, would play his mandolin and we would jump in the air and then fall on the shiny bunch of grapes, which would make the god of wine, Bacchus, go crazy. We continued jumping, and some of the children fell out of the cistern rhythmically like drunken bees.

All that movement stimulated our bladders, and I would immediately call my mother to help me descend from the cistern. I waited for every opportunity to be close to her, so much did I desire her attention and her caresses. She arrived like lightning and unceremoniously pulled me out, dripping *pipi* and *mosto* (grape juice) like a fountain, and without hesitation, she spanked me so naturally, as if this act was an integral part of the *vendemmia*. I began to cry and emit deafening sounds, less so for pain than for the humiliation of being beaten in front of the other children, who began to laugh uncontrollably. In that moment, I decided that I was not my mother's daughter but had been sold by the Gypsies to the Renda family. Gone forever was the sense of belonging, but notwithstanding it all, I wanted to belong to my family and consoled myself that there were at least five people who loved me dearly and were important to me: my Zia Maria, my custodian, my Zia Albina, who fed me bread and taralli, my father, who would always call me lovingly, and my sisters Gina and Nina. I adored Gina (two years older than I), who was not very good at school, and every time the teacher called her in front of the class to recite a poem she did not know, for her head was always some other place thinking how to help this or that person, he would ask her to open her hand and beat her with a stick while the other children counted till ten. What cruelty. What barbarism. I felt her pain and I would run in front of the class and stretch out my hand, imploring the teacher to hit me instead. I knew then that Gina and I belonged to each other.

At noon, everybody stopped working, Uncle Carmelo stopped playing the mandolin, and we all sat around the white tablecloth, woven at the loom by my mother, and abandoned ourselves to the exquisite foods my mother and the other women carried in big baskets on their heads. Famished as we were, we devoured the sacred banquet. Food was scarce but the women managed to make it look plentiful and festive by cooking peppers and other vegetables in many different ways. Ingenuity was a true gift from God.

Everything was harmonious and joyful during the *vendemmia*, and everything tasted better with a glass of wine from the previous year. We all drank with passion, as if it were the nectar of the gods. Then, the typical *pisolino* (nap) under the centennial olive trees, whose branches, moved by the welcomed breeze, refreshed our faces and souls. Lilla, my father's hunting dog, would lie next to him. Enveloped in this mantle of peace, we would fall asleep.

When the harvesting was finished at sunset, we returned home loaded, people and beasts. The donkeys carried their load with difficulty along the narrow and winding road, anxious to reach home to devour their hay. The women, loaded with baskets of fruits and wood for the fire, walked straight like statues; the least movement of the neck would cause their precious cargo to fall. Everyone was loaded except the men, who, cigarette in mouth, were still capable of whistling their favorite tunes. We, the children, were in front, jumping in the air as if we were announcing the theater of Harlequin and Columbine in the opera *I Pagliacci* that would take place in our piazza by a traveling group of artists every summer. Ours was a procession of tired people, but content that with the help of our Madonna, we had a good harvest.

Once at home, the *mosto* (wine juice) was poured into the cypress barrels built for the occasion by Nonno Luigi, and left to ferment for a few days, during which time we children would delight in watching this marvelous process of *mosto* turning into wine. The fermentation of the *mosto* seemed magical to us. We would stand there in front of the open barrels, watching the bubbles form in the depth of the barrels and then come to the surface like monsters spitting fire and emitting their last sounds, only to disappear and be replaced by others. I was enchanted by the whole process, by this transformation, which provoked many questions in my mind, but I did not dare ask questions, for everyone was very busy and not willing to give explanations.

I woke up from that vivid memory and saw Zia Maria bent over the grapevines with such love and tenderness that the vines had no alternative but to produce big, fat, sweet grapes next summer. But where would I be next year? Maybe in the belly of a whale, waiting like Geppetto, Pinocchio's father, for it to cough me out. I bent down to help Zia Maria finish tying the vines. As soon as we finished, she put the basket full of broccoli and other greens like chicory, dandelion and fennel on her head, and we began our journey home, followed by the goat, who had produced so much milk that her utters were full and ready to be relieved of their precious cargo, which, in the expert hands of my aunt, would become ricotta. I loved the impanata of ricotta, a mixture of serum, hard bread and ricotta, which we would devour seated in front of the fireplace chimney with the white hood. We enjoyed it as if it were our last supper; in fact, it was. Early tomorrow morning, my mother and I would leave in a black Balilla (car) for Pizzo, where we would catch the train to Naples, where Vulcania, the white ship, was waiting for us. Uncle Micuccio, who was present at my birth, would accompany us.

The image of Vulcania was omnipresent in my mind. I saw her everywhere; in the port, ready to cross the vast ocean, with music and passengers on the balcony waving to the relatives they would probably never see again. I would stand near my mother, who already sensed the movement even though the ship was still in the harbor. My mother's face did not announce a serene crossing. Poor me. I held tight my little creature newly found; I had given birth to myself; I felt complete. I saw my little village in the distance, unconscious of everything that was happening to me: I was going away forever from this land, its Romanesque cobblestone roads that had held me whenever I fell down howling with pain, bleeding knees, eyes moist with tears, but always more determined to march on in my wooden sandals.

My village, like Vulcania, was also omnipresent, but I felt it began to slowly vanish in the waters of the Atlantic. Perhaps it would appear in the profundity of the waters. I was waiting for the effect called "Fata Morgana," which would appear any time the terrestrial and heavenly conditions were such that the cities of Reggio Calabria and Messina, on opposite coasts, one in Calabria and the other in Sicily, would appear in the waters of the Strait of Messina and embrace each other in that eternal embrace of love; a perfect union of two entities abandoning their distinctness and becoming one. A metamorphosis devotedly wished for that appeared rarely. I was afraid that with my luck, instead of the Fata Morgana, Scylla and Charybdis (the two monsters, one on each side) would climb from the depth of the waters and bring us to their marine caverns to consume us.

My village, small and slumberous, buried in the sweet hills, between earth and sea, was not aware of my suffering, of my imaginings. Everything happened in my village. It was a microcosm of the bigger word that surrounded it but did not inhabit it. It was for me my universe, and now another universe was about to possess me. In my village, everything happened with regularity and normality: births, deaths, processions, sacred and funereal, marriages, dances and big meals in the open to celebrate the various harvests and the passing of the seasons. My eyes had seen it all: love, hatred, women loved and then abandoned, beaten and rejected when they were no longer useful to men. The bells sounded continually, announcing deaths; we knew exactly by the sound of the bells if the deceased was a man or a woman or a child by how many times the bells rang: three times for a man, two for a woman and one for a child. Even the bells knew the patriarchal order, I thought.

We all participated in the rhythm of the village; it was a chain that tied us, one to the other, in an unbreakable bond cemented by the clay, the hills, the trees, like the chestnut, maples, *l'abete* and the sweet olive trees, indispensable to our survival. They gave us the oil to make our minestras more delicious and nutritious. I owe my life partly to the olive oil.

My sister Nina, still preadolescent, knew the laws of commerce: a bottle of oil in exchange for a mouthful of milk from the breast of a wet nurse when I was days old. Perhaps we are created to live in small communities; in villages where it is only necessary to step out of one's comfort zone and empty oneself from the diatribes of living. There was always a little old lady seated in front of her house, ready to listen and give advice. These old ladies knew life well; they had lived every event life provided them with. Their wisdom came from personal and communal experiences; their hands had touched the profound abyss, and now they were ready to give help, to caress the wounds of others. I heard them tell sorrowful wives many times that marriages are not made in heaven but on earth by imperfect people, but advised them never to forget the power they had to manipulate events and circumstances in their own household. "Accept yourself as a stronger force than your husband; but remember, never try to dominate him."

13

The Lady Dressed in Black

I still had other people to see. I left the house in a hurry and went toward the house of Comare Maria, the lady dressed in black, to whom every night as a child I would bring a dish of steaming food. I would knock on the door and the usual tall, solemn woman appeared, wearing a long black skirt, a simple blouse and a kerchief, it too black, covering her small head. She beckoned me to enter her lugubrious abode. She lit the oil lamp and offered me a seat on an ancient chair made of hemp, it, too, showing the passage of time. I informed her of my impending departure; she solemnly got up, placed her long, venous hands on my head and blessed me as she always did when I brought her hot minestra.

I remained there for a moment to look at her; her serenity intrigued me, her chest flat as if they had taken both breasts away. (Years later when I had both breasts removed, my mother told me about Comare Maria, of her cancer in both breasts and how my father helped the doctor at the surgery, giving the patient grappa to knock her out. No anesthesia to prevent her immense pain.) I hesitated to leave; there was so much peace in that hovel with so little furniture, a small square table covered with a white tablecloth and two chairs around it. There were no signs of living things besides her, whose luminous eyes and serene countenance gave life to an otherwise lugubrious abode. She was the first minimalist I met.

I returned home, saddened by that solemn image of the lady dressed in black. I went to bed thinking of my Mimmo, and the many serenades he had played under our balcony with his beloved guitar. All those years I believed that those sweet melodies were for my sisters, who were beautifully developed; instead, they were for me, but I did not believe for I felt ugly, still very skinny with no semblance of a woman. I fell asleep to that evoked sweet sound and woke up at dawn, which announced a new day for everyone, but a tragic day for me, the day I would leave my dear abode, my whole world.

The fateful morning did not tarry; it came like a bolt of lightning. I got up, kissed my bed for the last time, said *addio* to the walls, which held not only our beds but olive oil, which was stored in huge clay jars situated in the niches in the walls. How much these sacred walls saw and heard through the century; how many earthquakes they withstood. I wanted to be strong like them and hold on to life and its tempests. I got dressed quickly, for time was marching on at an unusual speed. I hurried toward the kitchen and lit the fire in the fireplace for the last time to warm the milk, which my generous aunt had obtained from her beloved goat the night before. I made a good cup of coffee from roasted chicory, fresh ricotta with cornbread, and called my grieving mother to breakfast. We devoured all in perfect silence; even the fire stopped crackling. Words ceased to exist, for they were no longer capable of expressing our pain. We abandoned ourselves to that mystical, quiet moment, chewing our food super slowly, as if to prolong time.

We remained enveloped by that blessed silence till the sound of the Balilla coming to a stop echoed in our ears. Everybody, teary eyed, came out of their homes to wish us a good voyage. Uncle Domenico, with his luminous and warm smile, tried to lighten the funereal mood, but even he was not capable of infusing any joy amid the loud cries of us all. The Balilla left toward the zone called Sofone, where the ancient fountain continued its cantilena even during the bombing. Again everyone came out to greet us; among them Aunt Albina with a basket filled with taralli. I went toward the fountain to drink the last gulp of that blessed water that had quenched my thirst for seventeen years. The Balilla could no longer wait; we had a train to catch at Angitola.

We traveled in silence for about an hour, I, filling my

eyes with images of the countryside: the ginestra, the tall dry blades of grass (called *vutamu*) that caressed the path as they gently swayed in the wind. Some workers were harvesting it to make brooms, baskets and ropes. Nothing went to waste in our industrious village. Occasionally, a generous worker would make a thicker rope for us children, and we hung it on a branch of a big olive tree and spent hours swinging back and forth, trying to catch the delicate, lacy blossoms of these blessed trees as a gentle zephyr caressed them and made them descend to earth to leave space for the olives, still embryonic. As they fell on the brown earth, they graced the air with a magnificent perfume. The multitude of those minuscule flowers covered the earth with a white perfumed mantle. The entire countryside was an abandon to the senses, my paradise. Once again I got lost in that perfume, and woke to the sound of the train announcing its arrival at the station.

The trip on the train was very sad but also quite beautiful; its panorama was enchanting. The Tyrrhenian coast, with its white beaches like the flowers of the hawthorn bushes, meandered in my psyche like indelible sketches. Once again I lost myself in this idyllic scenery to lighten the heaviness of my broken heart. My mother, seated near me, was murmuring curses sotto voce to Christopher Columbus for not staying at home near his mother to gather olives instead of navigating the seas to find new land. We munched slowly on a panino that Uncle Domenico had bought at the Paola station, without uttering a sound.

The train arrived at the central station in Naples, and among the confusion, we managed to get the bus to the port where the long-imagined Vulcania stood, ready to welcome its new habitants. We gave our passports to a flashy sailor, all in white, and climbed the Vulcania, which we heard was on her last voyage. I was preoccupied, for I feared it was not capable of facing the legendary waves of the Strait of Gibraltar, which had swallowed and devoured entire boats. I had no other choice but to continue; a big line of people pushed me forward.

Once again I got lost in my anguish, which was becoming more palpable, and I hardly managed to stay erect. Another chapter of my life was about to begin. Would I be strong enough to face the challenge? I doubted it. At sunset, Vulcania left the safe port, with the band playing Neapolitan songs at full blast: "O Sole Mio," "Arrivederci Roma," "Torna a Surriento"… White handkerchiefs waved in the balcony, giving the last *addio* to the relatives who were becoming smaller and smaller as the ship got farther and farther away. My uncle Domenico was a point on the horizon. I remained there, surrounded by sea and sky, my panorama for the next thirteen days. Bitter, sad, silent tears inundated my being.

14

An Epic Voyage

The orchestra began to play, and all of the passengers went to the dining room, where an abundant supper was served: *spaghetti alle vongole, tagliatelle alla puttanesca*, followed by the *secondi*; *trippa* with tomatoes, *pollo alla cacciatora* and various vegetables, tomato salad with plenty of basil and panini of every shape. I had never seen so much food in my life, and recalling Nonno Luigi's admonitions to eat even if I vomited afterward, I began to devour part of that abundance with gusto, notwithstanding my pain. Baskets full of fruits followed, and then coffee and sweets. Everyone was eating voraciously. It was post-war, when hunger was still a problem. The Marshall Plan, envisioned by President Truman, helped us a little, for small quantities of food arrived in the South. Most of the food, however, remained in the North, where the greatest part was sold on the black market, perhaps some to the transatlantic ships, perhaps to Vulcania. My mother, still sick from the train ride and too sensitive to the movement of the ship, decided not to eat. I did not succeed in getting her to swallow a morsel. She, like Vulcania, had decided her course, she in not eating to avoid the discomfort of vomiting, the other intent to fight against the majestic waves that, like enormous arms, were coming from the depth of the sea to catch and devour their prey down at the bottom, where they lived. I had read *The Odyssey* and heard many stories about the sea monsters and how they devoured their prey. I was frightened.

The sunset was a spectacle though; the waters set on fire by the warm, last solar rays made us forget the anguish of the forced departure. My father insisted and commanded us to join him in Toronto, where he had emigrated a few years earlier, playing with our emotions, telling us that he missed us so much and suffered constantly, also promising that in three years we would all go back to our beloved village, where he had experienced the best and the worst.

The best was when he met my mother and decided to marry her, even against my grandfather's will, disobeying his decree that his daughters could not marry before age twenty-five, my mom being only twenty. The worst was during the reign of Mussolini, when, having refused to wear the black shirt, he was attacked every evening by some of Mussolini's thugs, taken in the dark to the river near which I was born, and after receiving a big dose of castor oil, he was beaten to the point of exhaustion, then left on the ground half dead. My mother, not seeing him return home, would go toward the river, an oil lamp to guide her, and when she found him she would bring him home, where he began to suffer for hours; castor oil was brutal. Her love, tenderness and care would bring him to life, only to see the whole process repeated the next night. We hated sundown, a reminder of what was to come. How brave and courageous my father was!

I began to think of my poor father and how hard he tried to keep us safe and fed. He would do anything for a kilo of flour: build gardens, farm houses... How ingenious he was when he built a tunnel in Serra San Bruno away from the German soldiers, he thought. There, among the majestic *faggi*, we would be safe. But the German soldiers went there before we did. It took my parents, sisters, grandfather and aunts the whole night to cross the hills and forests before we arrived at our destination. I was still a baby, barely two years old, but experienced our collective pain and remembered events with the lucidity of an adult.

One day my parents went out to forage for food and left all five children in the tunnel with strict orders not to go out. All of a sudden, we heard a loud sound and the roaring of a helicopter. My eldest sister Nina wanted to know what was happening. She ran out. We followed but the hellish flames stopped us. Nina arrived at the scene like a flash of lightning, and we watched in amazement as she pulled a body out of the flaming helicopter. She dragged him into our tunnel, washed him and put him behind the inner wall. My clever father had built an inconspicuous wall separating our living quarters from the rest of the tunnel. No one could tell there was a room behind the wall, a perfect design for hiding.

Soon we heard soldiers at the door of the tunnel. We pretended we were playing "Ring Around the Rosie," laughing and tumbling down like leaves. The soldiers came in and began to speak in a language we did not understand, looked the place over and yelled out, pointing their guns at us. My sister Nina asked them in Italian what they wanted and stood there in front of them like a *carabiniere* (a police officer), showing no fear. I was so afraid that I wanted them to go away. I went behind the curtain, took the chamber pot, which was full to the brim, and brought it to the soldiers, who, nauseated by that gesture, left the abode as rapidly as they had arrived.

Our parents came home desolate, without bread, only a few berries and dandelion greens. When they saw us trembling and looking down, they asked us if we had gone out. Pina, the most eloquent, told them about the man behind the wall. My parents brought the unfortunate one out, washed him, bandaged his burns and fed him what little food we had. We found out that he was American, flying the helicopter on a reconnaissance mission to see if German soldiers were still around. Sure enough they were there, for they shot down the helicopter and, seeing it in flames, thought that no one survived. This was the story my parents heard on the way to the tunnel. The unknown soldier stayed with us until we found out where the Americans were, and then my brilliant papa devised a plan. My mother dressed the soldier as a woman, big skirt, kerchief, and placed him on the donkey lent to us by a generous farmer. My sister triumphantly sat in front of him, and my father led them to the American troops, who were so grateful that in return they sent us tons of chocolates.

Still smelling and savoring those chocolates, I abandoned the memories and, together with my mother, descended the stairs leading to the depth of the ship, where a cabin with two bunk beds was provided. My mother, exhausted and filled with sadness, fell on the bed, finding refuge in sleep, which did not delay its arrival. I opened the door and tiptoed out in the corridor, and from the tiny window I stared at the waves which, with anger and furor, were pounding against the side of the ship, not unlike an angry mother slapping her child for misbehaving. Everything around was dark; I did not dare to go upstairs, afraid of getting lost. I was the type who feared everything; my sisters aroused my fears by telling me frightening stories. They narrated bizarre stories of dead people leaving their coffins at night to visit the village, and after walking all night, they reentered their tombs at the sound of the bells announcing dawn.

My father, a very courageous and fearless man, was known for having had multiple supernatural encounters. One early morning before dawn, he heard a knock at the door of our house. He got up in a hurry, opened the door and saw no one. He looked around and saw a shadow of a man descending the stairs and then disappearing into the void. He returned to bed waiting for the sound of the bells, then dressed and ran toward the church, where he assisted at the daily Mass as an altar boy before departing with the priest for a hunting expedition. Another time, he was coming home in the heart of the night, and saw an enormous fire lit under a grove of olive trees in our land, called Renda. He went near and saw a group of strange figures seated around the fire holding iron tridents in their left hands, laughing with such force that it shook the trees. Terrorized by the vision, he arrived at home trembling like a reed, unable to utter a word. My father, like me, had a reservoir of stories that lasted a lifetime.

Mine had not been an idyllic or serene childhood, but one filled with apprehensions, reprimands and fears. I was afraid of my shadow. However, nature was always near, my guide, my friend. I always found great comfort voicing my worries, my suffering, to the river, which carried them away in its gentle waters, where every anguish disappeared, becoming part of the greater sea. I would then feel light as a feather and sit on its banks, waiting for the answer to come in its gentle and constant murmuring.

I returned to the cabin and I, too, abandoned myself to the chimerical darkness of the night. The ship continued its course without any concern for our anguish. We were an insignificant point in the vast universe, but down deep in my heart, I believed that I was an important point in that universe, and felt best when I was in nature. I found every aspect of the natural world beautiful and healing. It was nature that helped me survive my rather traumatic childhood, and brought me to the discovery of many truths which formed and strengthened my being: such as the fact that we are all equal in the eyes of nature; we are all beautiful and belong to a race of great people who gave us music, art, sculptures, literature and a million other things. I was grateful for the little I had as long as I was in my beautiful hills and rivers contemplating greater things than myself.

Late in the morning we got up, and after great convincing, we went upstairs to an enormous room to have breakfast. Again a feast was before us: the traditional coffee and milk with ciambelle (ring-shaped cakes) filled with various marmalades, fruits and a basket full of bananas.

The first morsel I had of this delicious fruit was when

I was in middle school in Vibo Valentia. I lived in an apartment with my cousins Giovanna and her sisters and my mother, who took care of us.

Teresa with cousins Sara, Giovanna and Teresina in the garden of the house they rented in Vibo Valentia

Teresa's mother Angela (back left), Teresa (middle back) and cousins

Angela (back left), Teresa (front left) and cousins in Vibo Valentia

Across the landing lived a family of four in luxurious quarters with two children, a boy and a girl. The father was a wealthy merchant who had a shoe store on the *corso*, the most important street in the city. The girl was in grade one in a private school, but notwithstanding their wealth, she did not do well in school. The mother asked Giovanna to tutor her, but one day Giovanna was not available, and I took over. The girl arrived with a big banana in her right hand; I immediately began to salivate, and like the sudden eruption of a volcano, I grabbed the banana from her hand. The little girl began to scream at that barbaric act, but soon stopped after hearing my menaces and admonitions not to say anything to anybody. She dried her tears and we began the lesson.

I began to laugh at that remembrance, went to the table and filled my plate with bananas. I told my mother that with all those bananas I felt blessed. Bananas were a rare food after the war; commerce had ceased for those of us living at the end of the earth. My mother, on the other hand, barely ate anything.

The sky was limpid and rays of sun illuminated the long balcony, where passengers gathered in groups to discuss their lives. It was announced that the next day we would reach Lisbon, where the ship would anchor to pick up more passengers. The sailors, all dressed in white, would line up on the white balcony and Vulcania would make her great entrance in the harbor like a dancer on the stage. My mother and I were ecstatic to leave *l'ile flottante* (the floating island) and touch *terra ferma*.

But before reaching Lisbon, notwithstanding the blue and apparently serene sky, the sea began its dance, now slowly at a pleasant rhythm, then accelerating, one pirouette after another, each more and more menacing. The waves mounted the balcony with their diabolic strength, intent to devour everything on their way. They were the master of the ocean, we, an insignificant point in the universe. Miraculously, we made it to our cabin with the help of a sailor. Once we reached our cabin, he said goodbye and disappeared in the chaos.

As soon as I hit the bed, I began to vomit every ounce of banana, while my mother fainted on the bed with no sign of life. I attempted to bring her back to life, throwing more water on her already drenched face. I wiped her face and her body, removed the wet clothes, dressed her with the other set of clothes and put her on the bed, which was rocking back and forth like a pendulum. I crouched on the floor beside her with trembling lips, trying to pray that she would survive this horrid tempest. But the malefic waters continued their battle, becoming fiercer, hurling the ship against the waves, which appeared always more numerous. I was afraid the ship would break in two or that it would capsize, and we would all end up at the bottom of the ocean. I continued praying with the fervor of a child, but the tempest continued all day and night. Finally, at dawn, the waters became calm and there it was, the port of Lisbon in plain sight.

Breakfast was announced. My mother refused to go, but I, remembering my Nonno Luigi's admonitions to eat even if I had to throw up, went upstairs toward the dining room. I crossed the balcony, which showed no signs of the previous tempest. Chairs with the striped, harmonious cushions, sided by small round tables, stood there in perfect harmony. I asked myself if the storm was real or a dream. I only needed to look around, no people in sight. A man in uniform walked by; he saw me and came to a halt. It was the ship's captain. We talked about the storm and its violence. He told me that we crossed the point where the currents are usually so strong that many ships were swallowed whole by the waves. I began to tremble at the thought, but the captain soon realized my fears and assured me that that happened many centuries ago, when ships were not so sturdy and well built.

A basket of inviting bananas was at the center of the table. I avoided their glance but not their taste, feeling them still in my throat and feeling like throwing up again. I took deep breaths, like Nonno Luigi told me before the trip, and felt better. I ate hurriedly, in spite of the pleasant company, and went back to the cabin with a piece of bread and a cup of *caffe e latte* for my mother. I found her still in bed; I dressed her and we went upstairs to see Vulcania enter the port.

Vulcania was ready to let her passengers descend, and everyone, happy to touch *terra ferma*, hurried out. We had a couple of hours to walk around the port, full of curious people who came to see the sailors, impeccably dressed, lined up on the walkway. Holding my mother, who was still bewildered by the surging waves of the night, I descended cautiously, looking at the crowd that surrounded us like vultures. What did they want from us tired voyagers? My mother did not care; she had a plan.

15

The Escape

Taking advantage of the confusion around her, my mother took off without my realizing it. I looked around and did not see her. She was swallowed up by the crowd, so I thought. I began to cry and to call her. She could not have gone far; she could hardly walk. I went in and out of the crowd, but to no avail. Finally, exhausted, I asked a sailor for help. He took me to the captain, who recognized me and asked why I was crying. I told him and he immediately reassured me that we would find her and that Vulcania would not leave without my mother. He ordered a group of sailors to search the port. I followed them like a lost baby chick, and after a long search, seated in a dark corner of a little café at the end of the harbor, there was my mother, eating a croissant and sipping a cappuccino, content as a lark. She was wearing a kerchief, which she must have pulled out of her little handbag, and a pair of dark sunglasses as a disguise. As soon I saw her, I called her with a joyful voice of relief, but she did not answer. I ran toward her, and from the back, I embraced her and tried to give her a kiss. She pushed me away, saying: "Brutta bestia! you let them find me." She was not aware of my suffering; no one ever was. Only the river would listen to me and comfort me. How I missed my refuge.

The sailors tried to convince her to finish her coffee and go back to the ship, which was sounding the horn that it was time to sail. My mother remained unconvinced and told us to leave, for she had no intention to fight with the ocean any longer. She was happy in Portugal, where she knew a few words learned from my grandmother Dirce, who had been in Brazil. My mother became immobile, like the statue of our Madonna. The sailors, no longer patient, pulled her off the chair and she fell on the floor. She was so dramatic that I could see her on the stage; she was a performer. Two sailors grabbed her by her arms and two by her feet, and carried her out of the café and to the ship. What a spectacle! I became red like a peperoncino (hot pepper) with embarrassment.

With all aboard, Vulcania left the safe harbor and resumed her long journey on the Atlantic toward Halifax. We spent the whole day in the cabin; it was cold and windy. We were both closed in in an impenetrable mutism. I could no longer stand it and began to read the *Aeneid*, the only book I managed to bring; the book I had won in grade eight for reciting by memory "Lacrimae

Rerum" ("Tears of Things"), perfect for the occasion. My mother lay on the bed like a cadaver. I began to doubt if she would be strong enough to make it to Halifax. We had ten more days of oceanic rage. I imagined a burial at sea... I cast away that terrible thought and began concentrating on the first chapter of the *Aeneid*, which described the departure of the hero, Aeneas, from his beloved Troy in search of a new land, a new Troy. And I, what would I find in my new Troy, Canada? Would I ever feel at home like in Capistrano? Would there be swallows making their artistic nests under our eaves with such dexterity as to inspire architects and artists? I had spent hours watching them. My thoughts began to navigate the sea of who knows what I would find. Everything had become an interrogation point in my life; the only certainty I had was the fact that, after much searching, I had found that infant (myself), born to war, to despair, under a bridge. Emotionally exhausted, yet hopeful, I left the waters of uncertainty, and found refuge in the waters of memories.

16

A Tragedy

The image of my Zia Maria surfaced; she was a constant in my world of dreams and memories. In 1950, a tragedy happened in my young life. I was only eight years old when my muse, my love, began to show a bigger belly than I had seen before. I began to worry that she had a baby growing inside. I had seen many babies coming out of big bellies; even the Gypsies had babies. But in my innocence I had no idea how the babies would all of a sudden sprout into a belly like a cabbage, especially that of my beloved aunt, an ex-nun, a married nun. Was I responsible for that? Was I not enough for her? She loved me so much that perhaps she willed a baby of her own. I went to the river and told it about my aunt. The river listened attentively and murmured a rhythm of love and understanding, and I felt better.

Then I went home, and sitting on the doorstep, I saw our neighbor Stella with a big belly. How did she know how to make babies? When she got married, Gina and I worried that she and her groom did not know what to do. I knew what people did in bed. I saw it when I was three years old. My parents made love while I pretended to sleep. I slept in a small bed in their room until I was old enough to sleep with my sister Nina in the same bed. No one in the village talked about how babies are made; many talked about the laborious births. I walked around the village and saw so many women with big bellies, bellies everywhere. Why had I not noticed them before? They sprouted everywhere like mushrooms now. I reassured myself that Zia was not pregnant, for she walked straight and not bent like the others; perhaps she ate too much. However, the thought of what would happen to me lingered in my mind; first a passing thought, and as the days went by, it grew bigger and bigger in my head, like the newly discovered bellies around me. Yes, I had my parents, but it would not be the same with another baby running around. I would be dethroned and cast away.

I went toward Sofone, where I heard the Gypsies dancing and playing the "Anvil Chorus" from *Il Trovatore*. I met my mother coming home from the Gypsies' camp. She told me on the way home that she had helped deliver a baby boy, and the Gypsies were dancing and playing their instruments as the woman gave birth. I wondered if they would be dancing if a girl were born. My mother went on and on about the Gypsy woman and how beautiful the layette was. She probably stole every piece. I left her and returned to the river that went under the bridge and then divided into gentle rivulets singing away as they flowed through their journey. How I loved to watch them gayly dancing around. I sat on the banks of one and began my miserere.

I told the river that I loved my mother but at times I doubted I was her child. She was so happy to help deliver the Gypsy babies and enjoyed that the Gypsies welcomed the new life with dances and music. I too loved music; perhaps I was born like that in the Gypsies' camp, and I being a girl, they left me at my mother's doorsteps or in front of the nun's door. The river was silent; it did not answer me this time. The river knew more than I did or imagined. In fact, soon after, my Zia had a baby boy. He came amid screams that were heard through the hills; it was not the gentle melody of "Jubilate," but the agony of childbirth, of howling pain. I could not bear it as I stood in front of her house. My Zia had developed strong lungs with all the singing she had done in the convent, and kept howling for what seemed to me forever.

I gathered a bouquet of wildflowers growing on the riverbank and went toward the house to see the newborn. My Zia was in bed under white sheets; the smell of rubbing alcohol permeated the room, and a baby boy was lying next to her. I did not like this image. No one noticed my agony. No one comforted me. I left the room in silence, feeling the breeze caress my cheeks as it entered the room through the open fenestra. My world had collapsed. I stopped eating and no one noticed. With fifteen people at the table to be fed, food disappeared promptly whether I ate or not.

Fortunately for me, Mastro Antonio came and lifted my spirit with a performance of the "Anvil Chorus," in which my father participated by playing the triangles. Then he proceeded to tell us the story, which threw me into sadness again. Manrico, the main character, was not the Gypsy Azucena's child, although she raised him as her own. Manrico was the baby brother of Il Conte di Luna, and everyone believed he had perished in the fire. I totally identified with Manrico. I was not the real child of my parent either. I needed to find out who I was.

I finally decided to go to my paternal grandmother, Dirce. She loved me, I knew, and perhaps she would answer my question which no one in the village dared to answer. Solemnly, hands straight at my side, erect like a toy soldier, for I was short and delicate, I intoned my questions. "Who am I and who are my parents?"

"You are the youngest daughter of my Fineo, whom you look like. You are ours, not the nun's, and we all love you." No one ever asked why I thought I did not belong to my family. Everyone had quick answers which did not satisfy my thirst to know. We all need to know our own story of how we came into the world, who our parents are, in order to be grounded, to build an identity which will help us navigate our ocean. I definitely had an identity crisis until that ominous November day when my Zia and I went to Serra San Bruno to ask for protection from San Bruno, when she opened the gates of her heart and told me the whole story.

The Atlantic surrounded me, the sky enveloped ship and all. I thought of the aria "Cielo e Mar" (Sky and Sea) from the opera *La Gioconda*. I abandoned myself to that sweet sound that roared in my head like the waves that never ceased to crash with Vulcania. It seemed a continuous battle between man and nature; a nature in which her eternal rhythm demonstrated an invincible strength. I doubted we would make it to Halifax. Some passengers were saying that the ship was so old that it was her last voyage. Would it be my last one also? I wanted so much to live; I had many mountains to climb. It is amazing how our thoughts change, how we adapt to new circumstances, to new awareness. A few days ago Halifax represented an odious place for a village girl like me. Now I counted the days, hours and minutes until we arrived there and left the tormenting waters.

It was noon, my mother still in bed moaning, inert and lifeless. No longer able to withstand that sight, I asked her to tell me where that energetic, exuberant woman always in perpetual motion was. Hers was a life full of work; a day was long, laborious and varied: to Renda to gather the olives, then to Chiazzarello to gather the vegetables and fruits for the noon meal, and no sooner had she arrived home that she left again for the river to wash or rinse the clothes she had washed the day before in the same river, then hang the clothes on the ginestra bushes to let the sun or wind dry them. In the summer, the clothes would dry white as snow under the African sun. The sun was the best bleach, although my mother had already bleached and disinfected them the day before by pouring hot water mixed with ashes into a conical shaped vase with an opening at the bottom to let the water drain. Everything was recyclable in my mother's world, even the ashes. All this was accomplished by noon, back in time to prepare the main two o'clock meal.

In the evening after supper, she would furtively disappear downstairs, where, in an enormous room, lived the *telaio*, the weaving machine, a sacred object that was used to weave every form of cloth: sheets, blankets, silk for our dresses, shirts, nightgowns, sewn by the able hands of my mother with the machine operated by a pedal moved by her tired feet. My mother created cloth of such beauty, both in color and design, as to be worthy of a museum. I would stay there seated near her *telaio* by the light of the oil lamp, looking at her, especially her hands, with such ability and speed as they navigated the *navetta* (a canoe-like wooden tool full of thread). And my imagination became alive and saw the mouth of the *telaio* open and close to let the *navetta* deliver the threads from right to left, close its enormous mouth and then open to let the *navetta* go through again. The mouth of the *telaio* became for me a shark which, too, had left its world of the sea to know the world of the *telaio*, our world. I was never tired of looking at that marine monster's mouth close and open with the precision of a metronome. I was proud of my mother.

Finally, revived by my tale, she agreed to climb upstairs and join the other passengers to eat dinner, which was served Italian style, at one o'clock. Once upstairs, a sea of people met our eyes, all walking toward the dining room. We took our places, assigned to us the day we set foot on Vulcania, and began talking with our Capistrano friends—Nina, her two children, and two lovely young ladies from Bari whose father entrusted them to my mother. This time I passed on the bananas, the sensation and taste of vomit still in my mouth. My mother smiled at me, approving of my discipline. After dinner, satisfied and full, we went back to our cavern, our *refugium peccatorum*. The sea began to become agitated again; the sky was ominous, portent of another tempest looming. No land was in sight, only *cielo e mare*. Again I sang to myself the aria "Cielo e Mar" (Sky and Sea) from the opera *La Gioconda*, and immediately a calm came over me, enveloping my body in a mantle of peace. Music was always my comfort.

My mother, frightened by that diabolic rhythm, began to cry like a baby, uttering words of surrender and defeat. She was saying that she would not be able to withstand the journey, swearing at my father for having put her in this situation. Then she switched to Christopher Columbus for his inability to stay at home like a good son instead of going in search of other lands. I was the last in the series of blasphemes. I was the cause of her suffering; I, who wanted to study English, wasn't Italian enough? I felt equally angry, a victim in all of this. I was a minor and had no choice. We both were victims in following the command of the paterfamilias, who expected total obedience from his children and wife. I asked myself what would have happened if I had not submitted to the paternal will. Tired from speculations, I decided to embrace the present and make the best of it. I lay on the bed and began reading another chapter of the *Aeneid*, in which Hector descends to the underworld to consult with his father Anchises.

I, too, felt I had descended to the underworld, there in a cabin in the bowels of the ship, in the middle of an ocean unknown to me. Who would I consult, who was my Anchises? Maybe Nonna Dirce and Nonno Giuseppe, my paternal grandparents, who both, at the end of the eighteenth century, crossed the same waters that now surrounded me and frightened me with their gigantic waves. They, too, my ancestors, went toward an unknown land.

Nonna Dirce, obedient like me to the command of her father (my great-grandfather Leonzio), left her small town near Mantova with her family, eleven of them, for Brazil, where Leonzio would found a new empire, a new Troy for them all. How I felt for Dirce! How much anguish; how she must have suffered, fearful of an inclement sea, especially for us non-swimmers.

Notwithstanding the present difficulties, I was convinced that I, also descendant of these people, like them, would contribute to create a better world. This ancient force was in me to create, to live in full force. I felt in my veins the need to overcome the worst, live every pain that came my way and survive it all. I wasn't born under a bridge for nothing. Once I overcame the language difficulty, who would stop me? I saw myself as a big help to the immigrants, trying, like my great-grandfather Leonzio, to alleviate their anguish and helping them navigate the greater sea. I seemed to be navigating through my unconscious self. My thoughts and feelings were looking for a path back to where all rivers find the ocean. Perhaps I found mine in this ocean, surrounded by the waters of all my rivers, which have become part of this greater sea. I too would become part of a greater world like my ancestors who, tired of being rivulets, navigated toward the ocean.

The story of Leonzio was very much with me, and perhaps this was the moment to retell its epic voyage in writing, but the god of sleep took me in its comforting arms, and after a healing rest I woke to the sound of the supper bell. Upstairs, the band was playing Neapolitan melodies. We followed that pleasant sound and landed in a large dining room, where the tempest was far from our minds, and the crowd found comfort in eating, laughing and dancing the tarantella.

We ate and immediately after, my mother insisted we descend into the bowels of the ship, for unlike me she found no joy in dancing the tarantella. I reluctantly followed her toward the exit, having no idea why the hurry to go back to that dull cavern; perhaps she was feeling sick again. We lay on our beds; she closed her eyes and abandoned herself to her thoughts. I continued reading the *Aeneid.* At midnight, another tempest with water and wind made the boat swing from left to right in a perpetual motion. The boat was putting in a valiant effort to stay on course; the waves surrounded her, and at times it seemed like they wanted to swallow her alive.

My mother began to vomit continuously, and after a couple of hours, her stomach was totally empty and her body devoid of energy. She collapsed and I tried to wet her face with water, but without success. She was pale like death, and I began to cry loudly, hoping that someone would hear me and come in. After a long wait and no help in sight, I left the cabin and attempted to climb the stairs, hoping that upstairs there would be someone to help me. I swung like the boat, side to side, and a wave surrounded me and threw me down the few steps I had managed to climb and exposed me to the elements. Fortunately, a sailor saw me, and after a long scolding, he carried me to the cabin and took my mother to the clinic on the upstairs level. I followed them, swinging like a drunk. The doctor gave her some adrenalin to make her react and some saline substance. I remained near her all night till she awoke. She immediately scolded me as she saw me worried and crying. "Stop all this nonsense; did you think I would die? I will not die at sea."

We remained in the clinic till my mother was able to hold her food. We stayed mute; I did not want to talk so she would not get tired. The sea was calm now, but tempests are always on the horizon; after all it was November in high sea. Capistrano was becoming more and more distant and Halifax nearer and nearer. I was desolate but happy that my mother got better every day.

Not having anything to do, I decided to begin writing the story of my ancestors, who also experienced turbulent seas in their quests for a better life.

17

My Maternal Grandparents

My mother's parents were Luigi Florio and Marianna Pasceri. Nonno Luigi lived in his labyrinth on the first floor, and in the evenings, after supper, he would come to us, where he had a bedroom next to ours. We girls were fascinated by this colossal Nonno with a regal countenance and a smile which seldom adorned his lips. He loved to tell us about his youthful adventures, his trip to California in an ancient boat, where he experienced many tempests. He was twenty-five when he left Italy from Naples, the 24th of February 1905, and arrived at Ellis Island March 10, 1905. He was very moved to see the Statue of Liberty. "A woman!" he exclaimed. "The symbol of fertility and abundance!"

From New York he boarded a train for California, a train whose rhythm was slow but constant. It was a long trip and sometimes very boring, although it offered enchanting panoramas. He could not wait to reach

California, where he would be able to harvest gold from the rivers just like he did with olives from the olive trees. He was full of dreams; he would become rich and come back to the town, where everybody would admire him and pay homage to him by taking their hats off when he went by, greeting him as Don Luigi. But reality was different from his dreams. San Francisco was a crowded city filled with people just like him, who were in search of wealth. He met many Italians, with whom he would go to the rivers to comb for the gold that unfortunately was nonexistent. In the evening he would come back home with his friends, disappointed, but full of hope that the next day would be a more generous one.

One day he received a letter from his mother, Great-Grandmother Angelina, begging him to come back home immediately because she was at the end of her life, and she yearned to hold in her arms, for the last time, her adored Luigi. He, an obedient and devoted son, took the first boat available and left immediately. After two weeks of hell on a train, he reached Ellis Island. Not able to pay for the trip, he offered to work for the captain and was allowed to board a cargo boat where, anxious for his mother, he was not capable of abandoning himself to the benevolence of sleep. The trip on the cargo boat was painful. Every day feeding charcoal to the furnace, which would emanate a strong smell that caused him enormous headaches. Now and then he would abandon himself to memories of the cowboys with whom he lived for several months, and he would savor the long horseback rides in the Wild West. He loved living with the cowboys, who offered him a life free from any societal constrains, free to hunt and then roast the prey on an open fire which illuminated the austere surroundings, making them less menacing and almost lovable. He loved to listen to their stories, especially those of Edgar Allan Poe, like "The Tell-Tale Heart." Notwithstanding his poor understanding of English, he was capable of understanding enough to feel the constant and regular beating of the heart. In San Francisco he had learned some English with other Italians through courses offered by an Italian immigrant.

He arrived in Capistrano in the heart of the night after a month-long journey. His heart beat fast, just like in the story by Edgar Allan Poe, but he courageously opened the door which Angelina always kept unlocked for him and crossed the threshold, not knowing what he would find in the room. Slowly, he tiptoed to his mother's bedroom and saw her breathing normally. She opened her eyes and saw her Luigi. "I knew you would come," she shouted out joyfully and sprang up out of bed like a gazelle. Without wasting time, she lit the oil lamp and, pulling him by the hand, led him to the kitchen, where the tomato sauce was ready for the pasta. For the last two months, since she had sent the letter, Angelina would prepare fresh sauce every day, keeping it ready for his arrival. She lit the fire and began boiling the pasta—pasta riccia, Luigi's favorite. At first Luigi was very happy, relieved to find his mother alive and in great health, but soon he began to understand that his mother was about to give birth to a plan soon to be revealed to him. But the pasta riccia dressed with his mother's sauce, and a big glass of wine made by his father, were sufficient to dispel every suspicion from his mind.

Overcome by exhaustion, I fell asleep, lullabied by the ocean waves which, thanks to God, seemed less vigorous than before. I woke up to the enormous waves that, like giant sea monsters, were beating again against Vulcania. I thought of Nonno Luigi; how did he survive the numerous sea tempests? Maybe he lost himself in the smell of the furnace, which deadened his senses. I got up and looked out the little portholes. I saw a battle, two forces, man and nature. It was as if the sea would not tolerate intrusions and wanted to punish this boat that dared to cross its threshold. The moon illuminated everything from above, following its course in its orbit, showing her silvery face as if she wanted to say, "Nature is stronger than man; she has her laws and her eternal rhythm." I discovered early in life that we cannot fight nature, only abandon ourselves to her, and follow her commands with magnanimity and serenity, accepting her gifts as well as her furies. We need the wisdom of the Eskimos, who find refuge in their igloos and patiently wait for the calm to arrive. They are in tune with the elements and in harmony with the universe.

I was looking forward to meeting some Eskimos in Canada and, above all, holding in my hands their carvings, which spoke of beauty, simplicity and endurance. An immigrant who came back from Toronto once brought a little statue of mother and child and let the children of the village hold it. I never forgot the smoothness and the color of the soap stone. My hands were only used to holding rough clay statues which we dug from our earth and modeled.

The boat swayed back and forth like a drunkard and broke my reverie. There was nothing else to do but fall into oblivion. Where would I go to find refuge? Terrorized by those hungry waves, I left the porthole and walked to the cabin of my refuge and continued the story of Luigi and Marianna.

The day after his arrival, Luigi was convinced that his mother was not at the end of her life, but in full force. She would jump in and out of the kitchen like a cricket, bringing to the table first breakfast with coffee and milk, then fresh ricotta with figs and golden panini prepared by her nimble hands. She sat near her Luigi and announced to him with a vibrant but stern voice that today Marianna and her mother, Donna Maria, would come to pay them a visit. Luigi jumped to his feet and, with a menacing tone, yelled at her that he had no intention of meeting girls. He was not at the age of marriage. But his mother did not desist. She began the praise of the beautiful Marianna: a strong girl, well brought up, with the sweetness and candor of a Madonna. Besides, she was rich and belonged to a noble family. Luigi, no longer able to withstand this scheme, like lightning, left the house. But Angelina did not give up. She was as persistent as he was stubborn and immediately visited Donna Maria and Marianna, telling them that she and Luigi would be waiting for them at two o'clock for coffee.

At two o'clock mother and daughter arrived; Luigi got up to greet them but remained aloof and cold. Mother Angelina joyfully offered them coffee, which permeated the small kitchen with an aroma that lightened the heaviness of the moment. Luigi immediately announced that he would return to America, where his friends awaited him anxiously. "Then we must hasten the wedding," announced mother Angelina. Enraged, Luigi opened the door and ran out. Mother Angelina reassured Donna Maria that Luigi had a volcanic temper but once he calmed down, he would come to terms with reality. In fact, so it was. Soon after, Luigi surrendered to his mother's will and married Marianna. Angelina was convinced that once married, Luigi would renounce America and his wild projects. She firmly believed that women, apparently weak, had much influence on men, who, once married, would follow their wives like chicks. Women commanded the roost, but left the men to the belief that they were in charge. Whatever her philosophy, she knew that Luigi would never be a loving and faithful husband to Marianna; she also knew that he would bend to his mother's wishes. Thus, the beginning of obliged, arranged, and unwise marriages in our family.

Marianna and Luigi had a tempestuous marriage, but in the calm moments they managed to conceive eight children. Marianna was very religious, and every morning she would go to church before beginning her household duties, including taking care of the many properties she had brought to the marriage. Hers must have been a very difficult life, living with an unloving husband who spent most of his time blaspheming.

I imagine how many times she crossed herself when she went to bed with Luigi. Her faith gave her the force and strength to continue to live with a brute. She offered her suffering to Christ and found comfort in his example. But Marianna did not live long; hers was a short but exemplary life. She loved her children and was very much esteemed by the people of the village, except by Luigi's paramours. Marianna tolerated all his indiscretions with patience, even his failure in numerous commercial adventures, until her body could not keep pace with her husband's dreams to become wealthy, first in California, and now building roads in Capistrano. To obtain cash, he sold some of Marianna's property, where century-old olive trees produced oil in hallucinating quantities. Luigi felt strong and invincible, just like the Romans, and did not pay attention to any advice, much less to his wife's suffering. He was like a volcano ready to explode and destroy everything in its path. He had finally found his voice, after years of repression by a mother who hid her imperial strength under the guise of maternal love.

Unfortunately, his business enterprises totally failed, and Marianna fell ill after having lost her majestic olive trees, which were part of her being. Severe pneumonia took her away within three days. Useless were the hot compresses of flaxseed; antibiotics were simply not available at the time to the people of Capistrano. Marianna left eight children, the youngest of them, Antonio, scarcely two years old. My mother, already a young woman, tried to act as a mother to this little one who loved to go on bicycle rides, with her boyfriend, Fineo, who became my father. Albina, a four-year-old, went to live with Nonno's sister, Zia Micuccia, the weaver of the village. Poor little child; how did she survive the abandonment, first of her mother, who died very young, then her father, who took her away from the family hearth and left her alone with a widow, without the comfort of her brothers and sisters? To make things worse, her young brother, whom she adored, died a few weeks after their mother, Marianna.

Soon after Marianna's death, my mother dreamt of her mother, who announced to her that she would come to take her young Antonio. Two days later, the boy surrendered to an infernal fever caused by scarletina, a disease very common in our part of the world. Devastated by the death of little Antonio, my mother swore not to have children of her own, but to dedicate herself to her brothers and sisters, especially to Zia Maria, who was the most vulnerable to the tyranny of her father. Eventually, Zia Maria decided to abandon herself to the Carmelite Order and became a nun. After the novitiate, Maria was sent to France, where she had great difficulty learning the French language and made many gaffes. One night at vespers the nuns were reciting the Lord's Prayer, and Maria heard "pisciare" instead of "péché." She found it odd that the nuns were praying to be forgiven for urinating.

While Maria was struggling to make sense of a new language, Luigi, happy to have found his freedom, joyfully abandoned himself to conquering the beautiful ladies of the village. But his attempts failed miserably. The whole community, including his closest lovers, turned on him, even though he was the mayor of the town at the time and people tipped their hat when they met him. Yes, he had acquired the title of Don Luigi, but he had lost the esteem of the females in the village. No woman wanted him. He had abused the pure love of his wife. It was as if the women all came together to punish Luigi for his transgressions by depriving him of their love. His lovers, like the Greek women in *Lysistrata* (who locked themselves in the temple and refused to grant marital privileges to their husbands until they desisted to fight), refused one after the other to marry Luigi or have affairs with him. These were the first feminists of Capistrano, who demonstrated their solidarity and power against a predator.

Luigi began to live his long life of solitude, widowhood and abandonment until his death a few months before his hundredth birthday. But he did not surrender to his defeat. His strong and combative character surfaced, and he gave himself to creativity. He began building the first oil press close to the bridge where I was born. From November of every year, the olive press became active. We children were enchanted by the process of the olives becoming oil, a process we never grew bored of watching.

Here is how the olive oil was made. First the olives were put in a stone cistern around a great wheel which, propelled by the strength of the river's water, would mash the olives just like we children mashed the grapes with the force of our feet. The wheel went on and on, and would stop only after the olives had become a thick mash, just like bread dough; then the mash would be put in raw linen sacks that Zia Micuccia had woven on the loom and my mother had sewn. Once full, the sacks were put one on top of the other on a platform, under the press, extracting every drop of oil, which would fall into an enormous vat. Then a man with an agile and light hand would stand beside the vat and, with a brass disc plate also made by

Nonno Luigi, would gather the oil on the top and put it in clay jars. This was the virgin oil that everyone admired because of its greenish color and sweet taste. The word *virgin* fascinated me. Everything in our village had to be virgin to be good: oil, women, children dressed in white for the procession—and the men, were they virgin? I was confused but would not dare to ask questions. Virgin was a word on the lips of everyone, but discussed by no one. Everything became so mysterious in my little child's mind.

Olives were a sacred gift from God and every part of them was used. To extract more oil, heat was applied to the olive mash and then pressed. The resulting oil was catalogued as pure oil, which was used for frying, sauces, etc. The virgin oil was used for salads, minestre, pasta dishes and as a dip. We loved hot bread dipped in oil, garlic and a drop of vinegar graced by the sweet oregano we gathered on the hills.

Then more heat was applied to the mash, and it was pressed again. That oil was used to make soap, another magical event in my eyes. The mash, now dry as a bone, became a precious form of fuel for the fire, both at home for cooking and at the refinery to warm the place up.

The refinery had an enormous fireplace in the center of the room, and we children loved to watch those flames, which seemed to us eternal, emanating from that refined sand (the olive mash), which reminded us of the sand on the seashores. Besides, it provided a perfect place to bury potatoes and chestnuts and cook them to perfection. Everything seemed connected one to the other, to the senses and to our imagination.

Then the men would take a break from their toil and tell us stories, some sad that made us cry, others happy that made us laugh and many that made us scared. Our faces were like the Greek masks, one side sad, the other happy. We children knew we had descended from the Greeks; even our dialect had a lot of Greek words, and relics abounded around us. Greek discoveries were an archeological find, for they dated thousands of years ago when Calabria was part of the Magna Grecia, where Greek settlers had built cities and necropolises (cemeteries). Shipwrecks buried many treasures under the sea, and now and then the sea would cough some of them up.

For the first time I understood how important the olive tree was to our survival and what a privilege it was to wake up early and go to gather the olives after a windy night. There they were, waiting for us in the troughs which made the olive groves look like the lines of a notebook, straight and regular. He who had olive trees was considered wealthy, and my family had acres of them. I was fascinated by the stories about the olive tree told by the itinerant monks who would come down from the convents on the hills to beg for oil. In exchange for the oil, they would give us clay pots with big bellies made by them, which withstood a day of heat at the fireplace slowly cooking

MY MATERNAL GRANDPARENTS

beans and various minestre.

For me, more important than the clay pots were the stories they would narrate with such vivid gesticulation that every word uttered became cemented in my brain and stored for later conversation with my dearest friend, the river. One of these stories was about a Capuchin who brought the first olive plant to Liguria. He was sent there to found a new monastery, and in his cloth sack he put a piece of thick olive branch. Once he reached the location, he dug a hole and planted it. He watered it and cared for it with motherly love, until one day he saw the first branch with a few little green leaves appear. When he saw them, he became ecstatic and spent the whole day praying and singing praise to God. Liguria became one of the richest regions in olive oil production.

Another story that one of the monks gifted to us, for a story was always a gift to me, was that of a noble Calabrese woman who was a big supporter of the monks' monastery, on the hills not too far from her palace. One of the monks would visit her often to pray with her in the palace chapel. After months and years of these frequent visits, the countess got tired of seeing the Capuchin around and decided to remedy the situation. The monk began his narrative in a low, sonorous base voice. We children listened attentively.

"It was a tempestuous night; Fra Angelico knocked at the castle and as usual asked for the countess. He quietly and reverently entered the room, where a voluminous fire was sending millions of sparks through the chimney, and courteously greeted the countess, who, absorbed in her thoughts, did not appreciate the interruption. She made a sign for him to sit down, but Fra Angelico hesitantly asked: 'Your ladyship seems preoccupied, tell me what it is and like always I would be able to help.'

"The countess looked at him with obfuscate and malicious eyes. What was she hiding behind those blue eyes?

"Fra Angelico, very much devoted to the imperial generosity toward his monastery, decided to ignore his premonition and continued his visit in respectful silence. The countess called her servant and asked her to bring the usual pitta (a rough, round rye bread). Fra Angelico looked attentively at the servant, whose eyes, too, were hiding something. Without much ado, he greeted the ladies, left in the darkness and walked away toward the monastery.

"Once he arrived at the monastery, a tempest ensued. Trees groaned, bending to the wind, which mercilessly shook them, causing some to be eradicated from their beloved soil. Lightning bolts illuminated the monastery and the country around it; deafening thunders followed the lightning, and the monks began counting the seconds between lightning and thunder to calculate how far the lightning was from the monastery. Nothing was more frightening than lightning for the people of Calabria.

Accidents happened regularly, especially in places like the monastery, where towering trees surrounded it. They all fell on their knees as the lightning and the hail hit the roof, too close for comfort. They prayed that Saint Barbara, the patroness of lightning and thunder, would protect them and all those who were outside around the mountain.

"Amid the loud sound of thunder and hail which hit the roof with constant audacity, they heard an urgent knock at the door. Fra Angelico ran to open it and with an exuberant voice announced the presence of the *signorino*, the son of the countess, who, overtaken by the deluge, decided to find refuge with the Capuchins. They all invited him to sit down near the fireplace, where a meager supper was waiting. Fra Angelico pulled out from his mendicant sack the pitta he had received from the castle and invited him to eat it, for it was good bread.

" 'Eat, Signorino, bread made in your castle; your blessed mother gave it to me tonight when I went to greet her; eat it, it is fresh.'

"The *signorino* grabbed the bread and a salami that another brother had received, and without any regard toward the monks who were looking at him with envy, devoured it all with mighty speed. He was famished. The poor monks looked at that uncouth behavior and without uttering a sound, so great was their reverence for the countess, bowed their heads in prayer. After he finished eating, the *signorino* fell asleep, only to immediately wake up howling with pain and vomiting torrents. The monks tried to help him by giving him chamomile and a concoction of other herbal remedies, but to no avail. After many hours of torment, the *signorino* took his last breath. The monks became confused, not knowing what to do on such a tempestuous night. But Fra Angelico, notwithstanding the weather, decided to brave his way to the castle and inform the countess.

" 'What did he eat?' inquired the Countess.

"Fra Angelico, grateful that he was given permission to talk, spared her no detail.

" 'The *signorino*, caught by the storm, came to our monastery to find cover. Seeing that he was famished we offered him the bread that your *signoria* gave us. You should have seen how satisfied he was to find the bread offered to us by your benevolent hand. It was a joy for us to see him devour that holy bread. He also ate a whole salami that another of our monks received today. And then, after extreme pain in his stomach, he took a deep sigh and his soul went directly to heaven, light like a feather.' The countess, who of course had poisoned the bread, fainted, and when she came back to life, she exclaimed:

" 'Chi fa, fa per se.' " (He who harm others, harms himself.) That saying became part of our lexicon, on the lips of everyone, old and young. I adored the Capuchins; they pulled out of their sacks story after story to amaze us all. I loved to recall the many stories told to us by such skilled orators. But the bells rang; it was time for supper on the old Vulcania.

I woke my mother up and convinced her to come dine with me. The crowd was more subdued; everyone was eating slower than usual. Maybe the perpetual motion of Vulcania, the numerous tempests with their terrifying waves that mounted the boat like scared horses, had tired the souls of the passengers. A few danced the tarantella; I wanted to join them, but my mother pulled me by the arm and got up to go. Suddenly, a bombastic sound invaded the room, and we all stood still like marble statues. We all feared we would descend into the depths of the ocean and be devoured by the sharks. I ran to the chaplain, who was two tables removed, and asked him to hear my confession before the immolation. He looked at me with inquisitive eyes and asked why I was convinced the boat would go down; there was no tempest in sight.

"Excuse me Father, are you deaf? Did you not hear that horrible sound? Why haven't we heard it before?"

"Forgive me, Signorina, but in the last twelve days we have not had as thick a fog as this impairing visibility. Do you understand? And also, do not forget that we are not too far from Halifax, from the port, and there are many other boats around."

I was still so terrified that my mind was just as foggy

and missed the most important news, the proximity to the port. I saw nothing but death around me. We returned to our cabin, and I thought I should confront my mother on the events concerning my birth, but looking at her sad eyes, I did not have the courage to add to her distress. Again I abandoned myself to the story of my ancestors, losing hope to ever find the right moment to confront her.

18

The Arrival

After thirteen days of tempest and terror in high seas, we were able to see land. Vulcania began to approach the port of Halifax. With difficulty due to the fog, we were able to see the people waving handkerchiefs; no one was waving them for us, two pathetic figures, a poor semblance of women, hardly able to stand erect. We disembarked by walking on a *passarella*, all trembling like us. The constant movement caused my mother to fall into the icy waters, and I, trying to pull her out, followed her in. Fortunately, a sailor saw us and jumped in to fish us out; otherwise we would have drowned, given that we were both non-swimmers. Another sailor accompanied us to the receiving room and gave us towels to dry off with. We were soaked and cold.

We boarded the train that was waiting for us and began the voyage toward Toronto at a snail's pace. A fierce cold penetrated our bones, and our teeth began to chatter uncontrollably. An attendant took pity on us and gave us a blanket, with which we covered ourselves up to our faces, trying to breathe out to create our own warmth. But the teeth continued to chatter; it seemed they had found their own rhythm, guided by a force outside us. I was afraid that my mother would fall sick again, and two big, furtive tears rolled down my face, already marked by an arduous voyage.

Through the window appeared faraway villages with tiny houses, their roofs covered with snow and their chimneys emitting into the icy air a warm smoke that I imagined would penetrate my body. Who knows what their habitants were doing on such a brumal day. In my thoughts I tried to cross the ocean in order to find myself in front of my brazier listening to the operas narrated and sung by Mastro Antonio, but the images of the marine tempests were too frightening still, and I was obliged to remain in the present, immersing myself in those little villages that ran one after the other like rabbits, playing with sun shadows now lengthening, then shortening. ultimately vanishing in the white snow. I saw wild rabbits covered with a white mantle used as camouflage in that colorless, candid environment of snow that was not in a hurry to dissolve at the light and delicate touch of the autumnal sun. I had no knowledge of how long the snow lasted. I felt like I was at the North Pole, but I tried not to tarry in this gelid vision, so as not to begin shivering again.

All the passengers slept, lullabied by the monotonous

rhythm of the slowest train I ever experienced. My mother and I became part of that somnolent scene. I dreamed that I was at the opera house watching *La Wally*. The theater was a sea of snow where La Wally, the heroine by the same name as the opera, was running on the white snow, singing her doleful aria:

Eh ben, ne andro' lontana come il suono della pia campana.
La fra la neve bianca, la' fra le nubi d'or,
Laddove la speranza e' rimpianto ed e' dolor.
(Yes, I will go far away, like the sound of the sad bells.
There among the white snow, there among the golden clouds,
Where hope is regret and sorrow)

The train stopped abruptly and shook me from my dream. We were in a small station unknown to me; there was no name. I took advantage of the stop and went to the bar to buy some bread and hot coffee. In the confusion at Halifax, we did not receive the package of food for the trip. Unfortunately, the bar could not offer much: a loaf of bread as white and soft as the snow, sliced in squares perfectly symmetrical, and wrapped in a plastic bag with the name Wonder Bread. The attendant offered me one and a can of meat called Spam, with two coffees in paper cups. I rushed back to my place before the train moved, where my hungry mother was impatiently waiting. She saw everything I brought and began to yell at me, saying that she still had teeth and did not need this awful soft bread. Bring it back and ask for some *pane decente* (decent bread). I, most of the time docile and understanding, decided to protest that I did not know how to say "pane decente" in English. But she, like a recalcitrant child who does not listen to the voice of reason, grabbed my hand and put my fingers on my teeth, saying, "Show them to whoever is there."

I hurried toward the café and showed the attendant my perfect white teeth. He burst out laughing and I, red as a peperoncino, returned to my seat, bread in hand. I consoled myself that sometime soon we would reach Montreal, and being a big city, there would be vendors at the station selling panini with "decent" bread. I imagined it would be like a train station in Italy. However, hunger possessed us, and in silence we began to eat the bread with the Spam, a cold marbled meat resembling a white and grey mosaic. We swallowed with difficulty and even drank the coffee which, according to my mom, was brown, dirty water.

After many hours we arrived at the Montreal station, where a pleasant surprise awaited us. My beautiful sister Pina and her husband Toto were there waiting for us with a basket full of every food known and dear to us. I saw them first, but afraid that my mom would exit the train and refuse to board it again (Lisbon was still fresh in mind), I decided not to wake her up. My sister came into the compartment to see her, sleeping deeply like a newborn baby.

My sister descended, and the train slowly but steadily moved out of the station. I, at the window, followed the image of my Pina as it dissolved in the ether, sad but joyful to have seen and embraced my *bambolina* (little doll), the name they gave her in the village for her beauty and fragility. I abandoned myself to the monotonous buzzing of the train and began visualizing our home in Capistrano when we were all together, the five of us, living an idyllic life in spite of the war. How ugly separation is! Embracing my Pina seemed like embracing a stranger, not a dear sister who used to embroider my dresses to hide the holes in the cloth. I was always an ambulatory garden, flowers in the front, in the back, on the sleeves, flowers everywhere there was a tear to plant them. And I was the happiest little girl, thanks to those nimble fingers. My Pina was the master of embroidery.

One summer I was invited to go to Reggio Calabria to visit my uncle Ottavio and his new bride, Nella. Pina, happy as a lark, began to make me a blue silk dress with strawberries on the border. They were so real that I began to salivate every time I saw the dress. The whole family was happy for me. I experienced that communal joy whenever something good happened to one of us or someone else. The beauty of living in a village where every joy or sorrow was shared because we had bonded due to our interdependence was mostly felt during the war. Perhaps the war had taught us something valuable, in its macabre way.

The morning of my departure for Reggio, Pina fixed my hair, making curls with the curling iron given to her by one of her admirers. No one was willing to subject herself to that curling iron, which, after hours on the hot coals, became so hot that it could, at a minimal touch, burn the scalp and send you howling. I, being the youngest, was the chosen victim offered in the name of progress. I would end up with a massive curl which sat in the middle of my head like a porcino mushroom. After innumerable screams that came out of my mouth at full force, I would look in the mirror and become proud of my mushroom, and strutted in front of everyone like a peacock in my shiny blue silk dress. The little girls of the village envied me, while the little boys would make fun, calling me *porcina* (little pig).

I ignored every mockery and refused to look at them, total detachment from anything negative, an art that I was able to perfect as time passed and the insults continued. Detachment became one of my techniques of defense and survival in a world where laughter and tears, comedy and tragedy, love and hate intersected each other like the lines of the cross. I learned very early in life that children, notwithstanding their angelic faces, can be very cruel. I vowed never to be one of them. I'd carry my cross without inflicting pain on others and learn to survive joyfully and patiently. I had my companion, my comforter, the river, which carried me to wonderful worlds of dreams and enchantment.

It took us several days to cross Quebec into Ontario in order to reach Toronto. We entered the Toronto station late in the evening and ventured toward the exit, following the leader like a herd of sheep. I was a little apprehensive to meet my father after many years but tried to keep calm and unemotional. My mother looked indifferent and comatose, but I, as always, tried to remind her that in the waiting room, her beloved Fineo was waiting for her. She shrugged her shoulders and remained as mute as the statues in our church back home. We reached the enormous waiting room; my father saw us and ran toward us with open arms. His eyes glistened with joy to embrace his family after years of separation. After having retrieved our two cardboard suitcases which, notwithstanding their fragility, had survived a tumultuous voyage, we walked outside.

The cold was palpable and my mother and I, not used to such brutality, began to tremble like leaves. Enormous lamps illuminated the sidewalks, and an imperial and marmoreal building, adorned by huge glass windows capable of impressing even the architects of the Antica Roma stood silent across the street. That building remained a symbol of survival for me through the years, my survival in an icy land.

My father's friend Giacomino, an immigrant from the North, was waiting for us with the car. We traveled on University Avenue, a long and wide boulevard flanked by numerous enormous buildings, with roofs covered by newly laden snow; what an enchanting panorama! I was fascinated and looked intently, filling my eyes with wonderment after seeing the minuscule houses from the train for three full days.

Then we turned onto Harbord Street, and along its winding road we saw the University of Toronto with its many colleges. Even under the snow they looked enticing. Would I be able to go there some day? We turned left onto the road Montrose where my father and sisters lived. When they saw the car, they ran out and the hugs and tears began and lasted for many days. We were very tactile, my sisters and I. What joy to see my Nina, who had carried me in her arms looking for a wet nurse through the arduous roads in Capistrano. And my Gina, with that round, luminous face like the sun, which shed light and warmth upon everyone she met. She was total goodness; she was sent to us by God to lend a helping hand to the living and the dying. My Gina was the first to answer the sound of the bells announcing the death of a villager. Gina and I were very close, a year apart, and we shared our thoughts, our joys and our work. We were inseparable. I could not wait to go to bed and share the events that happened during our years of separation.

We slept on the pull-out bed in the living room, near the kitchen; my parents slept on the third floor. I went up the stairs to accompany my mom, and when we reached the second floor, we both slipped and found ourselves in the kitchen of the renters. Surprised by the unexpected visit, they remained there like statues, but once the shock passed they helped us to get up. I guess we were not used to shiny, waxed, wood floors. My whole family ran to help, and the little kitchen became a hive of buzzing, for everyone talked at the same time, each with a different explanation. There was nothing to explain, but we were all Italian and we never got lost for words. We descended from the Romans, whose specialty was oratory. My family apologized profusely for the interruption, but no apologies were necessary; instead, we were all offered a glass of wine, cheeses and sausages to celebrate our arrival. It reminded me of the story of the lady in Rome who, being depressed, opened the window and began to yell out that she was about to kill herself. The people going by stopped and began to talk to her about their conditions. The suicidal lady, tired of listening to their stories, invited them to come up and have a dish of spaghetti with her. They all went up and ate and drank the whole night, and no one talked about death.

We continued our journey to the third floor, one after

the other, a procession of happy souls. My mother had no idea where she was, after a long, exhausting trip and the fall. We put her in bed and forced her to drink a cup of warm milk with coffee. My mother loved *caffe e latte*. She drank it all without any effort, then tied her customary kerchief on her forehead and signaled for us to go. She needed her peace and quiet. We descended the stairs silently like mice, and we sat to a sumptuous meal in the basement. The crusty bread prepared by our Nina was for us the most appreciated food, then an array of risottos, *pastina in brodo* and cutlets, stuffed eggplants, all the food my mother and I loved; what a shame she was not sitting with us.

Mealtime has always been the most important point in our family; even during the war when food was scarce, we always managed to eat in style. I remember most vividly the pasta and beans, whose aroma knocked us out. We always had an unannounced guest, and we all gladly shared our portions. Now our Nina recreated the same ambience with more food, without the unexpected visitors. We lived in a big city now where anonymity would reign supreme. I already missed the coziness, the familiarity of the village, where everything was shared and enjoyed or cried about together.

I looked at my father with more love and understanding. How he must have suffered in his first years in Canada. I wanted to embrace him and tell him that, notwithstanding our treacherous journey, I was glad to be with him, but I was too emotional to say it all calmly and composed. Instead, I remembered his heroic acts in Capistrano when he arrived home one afternoon and brought us Peppina, the mentally challenged young girl whose parents, not knowing what to do with her, committed her to an insane asylum. My father went to the asylum to see her, and seeing the horrible conditions Peppina lived in, he decided to convince Peppina's parents to bring her home. The parents were not happy, but no one in the village could say no to my father, the great benefactor. Peppina was so happy that she would go around the village and narrate the story of how Master Fineo told the director: "Peppina cannot stay here in this place where the name alone strikes fear, Cilifarcu." Peppina loved us Renda girls, and if anyone dared to hurt us or say something bad, she would throw them on the ground and beat them. She had Herculean strength. We all loved her and she ran around joyfully singing and chirping like a bird.

We continued to eat and drink the wine made by Rocco, Nina's husband, and my father. They would buy grapes and then use the same procedures they did in Capistrano to make the precious wine in the backyard. They brought with them their customs and tried to recreate the way of life they left behind. I, too would become the sustainer of many of our traditions.

I was in awe of how much food I saw in one evening. All kinds of fruits from Florida, California, and God knows where else. I was born during the Second World War to hunger and uncertainty and grew up post-war, when few provisions arrived to us from the USA through the Marshall Plan. The bulk remained in the North, some distributed to the citizens, the rest sold on the black market. The Americans were very generous; it was our people who cheated us. The Americans sacrificed a lot for all of us; if it weren't for those valiant young men who lost their lives for us, Hitler would have destroyed all the people of the South, from Rome down. We were not blue eyed with blond hair; we were not part of the master race, but disposable nothings.

My beloved Gina and I slept on a sofa bed in the living room. We had so much to share, but she had to get up early for work the next morning, and she decided to try to fall asleep. Fortunately for me, I was so tired that I would not have been able to formulate a coherent thought anyway. I woke up to a quieter house; everyone had gone to work except my sister Nina, who stayed home with her baby Michele. We had our continental breakfast, and seeing that the sun was shining, we decided to go out and explore Little Italy, where incredible events were waiting to happen.

Epilogue

A Gentle Death
Written on the tenth anniversary of her death

Mother on her deathbed.

The candle flickers. Just the two of us. Mother lying on the bed motionless, I beside the bed, watching her for any sign of life. Is it the death she wished for? Lying peacefully, breathing gently as if in a deep sleep. Her face calm and serene, becoming whiter but still possessing the pink tinge that made her skin beautiful. I could not detect the pallor of death. Just the two of us. The candle still burning, casting a shadow on the wall. I, too, am in the dark valley of death.

"No, she is not dying. This has happened before." Father Janvie gave her the last rights, and then she woke up. No Father Janvie to call on now; perhaps he is assisting a Cameroonian woman to cross the threshold. How my mother loved Father Janvie. She would say:

"Cook him lots of pasta, he is hungry. No, no, add two eggs in the pasta like his mom used to do. He needs a lot of strength to deal with all those demanding parishioners." Both she and Father Janvie came from a little village, and like him, she felt a foreigner in a land of abundance but a spiritual desert. I would not dare to call a priest from the parish we belonged to. She needed her little African priest, with whom she felt an affinity.

Perhaps because they both had to go a long distance to fetch water for their daily needs. A long way it was from the village to the river, the rivers near them dried up. In Cameroon, when the French cut down the rubber trees to make tires, the deforestation began causing the river near Father Janvie's house to dry up, consequently depriving him of the opportunity to go to school, for it took him the whole day to go and fetch the blessed water. My mother's river dried up when people who had property above hers rerouted the water of the river that flowed through her property.

The candle continued to burn but flickered more steadily, announcing its end. My mother's body did not flicker; no movement except the chest still able to rise and fall as the breathing continued.

"Pray, sing. Don't lie there like a rock." Her voice in my mind truncated my thoughts. I began to recite Psalm 23: The Lord is my Shepherd.

"Memorize them, for when the day comes, you will

not be able to find your glasses and I will go without hearing them," and then she would laugh.

She laughed a lot in her last years; before, she had no time to laugh, only to work. Her hands were never at rest.

I began to recite her favorite prayers and sing her favorite opera arias. I wanted to say: "Mom, am I doing a good job?" I always wanted her approval, no matter how old I was. How I wished the wise old ladies of the village were there with us, keeping the death vigil. I missed their voices, their monotonous cantilenas. But I was alone; only the candle kept me company, casting its shadows on the wall. "Mom, I have something to ask you, a secret which has been buried in me for a long time." I wanted to tell her that. Instead, I heard her admonition in my mind. "Continue reciting the 'Salve Regina'… Sing, sing; why did God give you a voice?" The words rang in my heart like the church bells. Sixty-four years of living and I have never been able to mute her voice within me. It was part of my fiber.

I need to talk to you, Mother. Perhaps to reenter your womb and come out chirping to the sun like a little bird. No darkness, no bombs, not under a bridge, but born in bed like every other child, born to joy and love. I need to talk to you about the circumstances of my birth, a secret I have carried since 1958, a day before we left our beloved village. I spent the last 57 years waiting for Godot; for the perfect moment to tell you my side of the story and hear yours. I have the right to know, to be born again into a world of love and not indifference; of acceptance and not rejection. I need to find the truth to dispel the stories I created, which have grown to monstrous proportions and become too heavy to carry on my journey. I wanted to say all this, but...

Unfortunately, I waited too long for the perfect moment; this is not the perfect moment either; only a cruel moment if I were to unburden my soul when you have no chance to respond. I love you too much to be cruel. I am seeing now that there is no perfect moment, only moments to seize and live fully.

Let me recall instead the joyous moments, the warmth we felt when the American soldiers passed by our village, marching through like gods, dipping into their pockets and bringing out handfuls of chocolates. At that moment I wanted to go to their land of chocolates; you pulled me away as I wanted to follow them, but they disappeared as fast as they came, afraid they would be infested with lice. But they stayed long enough for the lice to jump from our heads to theirs.

The next day, a helicopter circled over our village and spread a liquid with a pungent smell on our houses, gardens and everyone caught outside. It was a beautiful sunny day with clear skies, and all of us children were outside playing our usual games. At first, we loved the "rain" coming down steadily as a mid-afternoon shower.

A GENTLE DEATH

You came to the window and asked us to come in. When you smelled us, you knew it was DDT, and so bravely took us to the river to wash us up. You had just come from the river with a load of wet clothes in a basket ready to be disinfected overnight with hot water and lye made from ashes. I never forget your tenderness; you knew this time we did nothing wrong. We were victims of the war that brought us lice, famine and destruction.

The next day, the same helicopter circled over our houses. We immediately went indoors, still smelling of DDT. We saw white sheets of paper pouring out of the helicopter. We ran outside. The sheets of paper kept descending over our heads like olive blossoms on an August day... We danced; we welcomed the bountiful new rain; we needed paper, a rare commodity. We gathered them as carefully as we gathered the olives and brought them in to be read:

SPRAYING THE VILLAGE AND THE COUNTRYSIDE WITH DDT TOMORROW TO DISINFECT. KEEP CHILDREN INSIDE.

Everyone in the village who knew how to read read and reread the message, which did not make sense; they had already sprayed the day before, but you announced to us that we should stay indoors the next day. Then I knew that you loved us, me included, for you wanted to protect us from harm. But wasn't the harm already done?

My eyes were getting heavy; it was well into the night. I could hear my husband snoring in our bedroom. I got under the covers; both of us now under her wedding bedspread, still white as the day she got married. I knew she loved it, for it was one of the few things she carefully put in her cardboard suitcase before sailing away to another world. The candle gave its last gasp and left us in the dark. I took her hand, still warm, and kissed it as it became moist with my tears.

Alone, the two of us; I waited for sleep, a sweet, regenerating sleep, to embrace me. I was prepared to stay there beside you; I was not going to abandon you again as I did when I moved to the USA. You suffered a great deal then, being in Toronto without me; we had grown accustomed to each other.

There I lay, beside this wonderful being whose life had been majestic once, and now was slowly becoming a corpse. Silently, I lay there with a heavy heart full of regrets. Why didn't I tell you then, when I came back from Serra San Bruno, after my epiphany? I ran to you; I wanted to take you into my arms and hold you like a mother holds her baby; fill your face with kisses and call you Mother like I had not done before. My valiant mother, I forgive you for not holding me close to you when I first gasped for air.

No, I could not tell you then what I had learned from my muse, Zia Maria. You were sitting among your friends in the dining room. You were all somber, dressed in black, mute like the saints in the church staring away into the darkness that began to envelop you. Night had fallen over the village and on every broken heart. Although you remained silent as in a funeral dirge, no one had the energy or will to go on. I could not disturb your mourning; perhaps the last time you would spend together with these blessed women who helped you to bake bread when at the age of ten, your legs could not reach the oven. The big oven in the wall which devoured like a hungry lion all the bundles of wood you brought down from the mountains on your gentle head and your legs trembling like a reed, week from hunger.

You needed that intimacy with them; that silent communion, an evening of recollection to ease the pangs of separation. How brave you were at the age of fifty to leave your world. A world where you had learned how to walk amid soldiers; how to survive the deprivation of a loving mother's hand. A world of hell, left alone with ten brothers and sisters and a father whose commands and edicts sounded louder than the church bells. Yet, it was the only world you knew. How can one leave a world we know for something total alien?

Remember our second day in Toronto, when we walked, by mistake, into an Italian movie house hoping to see a Fellini or an Antonioni? Instead, a stage full of naked men appeared. I began to scream at the sight of all those dangling penises. I had never seen one, and probably neither had you. We were all conceived in a dark room where your bedroom was; no electricity, no oil lamp. I, the virgin, had never dreamed of seeing one. I had a glimpse of one when our beloved Ciccio peed out of spite on my violets in my little garden.

Your roar was heard all around, as was your admonition: Teresa *chiudi gli occhi*! (Teresa, close your eyes!) The owner, like a flash of lightning, escorted us out, filling our hands with money. We entered a Jewish bakery next to the movie house. We wanted to find comfort in a loaf of shiny bread. We bought two challahs, one each, and left arm in arm, eating and laughing. Our first encounter with sweet bread; the daily assault on our teeth began and continued for years. Your love affair with sweets and decay continued until you lost all your teeth. Fortunately, I escaped the carnage.

Now I understand the malevolence of war. Remember when you came to Fort Knox, Kentucky, to visit us (Tom, my husband, had been drafted into the army), and saw some of the soldiers who had just returned from Vietnam, wounded and maimed, with others trembling when the four o'clock levy was announced? You cried as we ate our first chili dog in the cafeteria, seated next to some of the returnees. You, too, were maimed by the remembrance of the war, climbing to the mountains at night, pregnant, with a two-year-old holding on to your skirt. How frightened you must have been in the dark, thinking that every tree was a German soldier ready to shoot. The war still haunts you, that war that brought you famine, destruction and two baby girls.

The moon was still shining and lit my Japanese garden, which looked divine under its spell. I had to get up, go out and breathe the air of the living. I walked from one garden to the other, each created with a specific purpose in mind; each had to perform a miracle upon its completion—to heal my cancer wounds. I sat there on the wooden bridge over the little dry river, and as I looked intently, each stone became a living drop of water taking me to my hills, to my beloved river and *la ginestra*—to Serra San Bruno, where I took my first steps on that imperious yet humble staircase, each step made of cement which endured the bombs of the Second World War, leading us to heaven, to our shelter where the enemy could not reach us. We lived in tunnels dug with care by the strong men who refused to wear the black shirt.

As I looked to the majestic Russian olive tree at the end of the bridge, my thoughts went to our oil refinery, to the hellish fire that burned forever; a different fire made not of flames but of brightly red and blue olive mash burning without end, without assistance. A mound of sand on fire. The men singing and, with a big flat ladle, gathering the precious oil that came up to the surface of the vats and effortlessly separated itself from the water.

"Oil and water do not mix," Aunt Beth used to say whenever she saw two young people from different classes in love. I never understood Zia Beth; both are useful and indispensable to the miracle of life. Who was the oil, who was the water? Many times I wanted to ask Zia Beth to explain, but I was obsessed with finding out who I was, who my parents were... Why no one wanted to talk about my birth. Was I adopted or was I the daughter of a Gypsy, one of those men who would come to sell us tripods? Impossible! My mom always had a headache.

Seventeen years of waiting, the day before we left for Canada. One voyage of discovery ended that Friday. My Calvary was over. But alas... the next day I was to embark for another voyage in the land of unknowns; where I would have to become a child again and learn to talk, to put my tongue between my teeth and blow out the cursed "TH" in front of a candle. If the flame flickered, I was almost there, ready to pronounce the words this, that, there etc.

I could have stayed on the bridge under the old chestnut tree; the moon rays lighting my white nightgown—I felt like a nymph, a breathless nymph. I touched my breasts; they were not there. I felt empty, like a newly tilled field ready to be planted. Sitting on the bridge, being immersed in the waters of my blessed river, my new Baptism, washed clean from my diatribes. I felt no cancer. The water had washed away every malaise and emptied it into the big salty sea to salinate every drop and blend them together to make the web of life. I felt free like I had never felt before: no longer obsessed by my regret of not having confronted my mom regarding my birth; I had emptied my soul to the chestnut tree, washed my sins in the cleansing waters of the stone river; I was ready to see the world anew, light as a feather.

I walked silently and reverently back in. I had no need to tell her anything about my anguish, only remember our journey together. I told everything to the chestnut tree; I entered now to celebrate a life well lived in spite of the myriads of impasses that she had encountered.

I took my place beside my living corpse; my beautiful mamma, serene in her own world, in her silence. It is interesting how silence has its many hues: the silent embrace of two lovers full of promise of a world together; the silence after hearing an opera—the words, the story, enveloped in the still vibrating notes edged reverently in our psyche. The silence of the tomb. No one walks through a cemetery dancing and skipping to the sound of the flute. Even its delicate sound would be an annoyance. Only children can do that, for their minds are not constantly bathed in sorrow; they live for the moment, the moment of joy.

In the silence of this night, I was watching my beloved trying to cross to the other side. She had prepared for this moment her whole life. Every day I heard her pray for a good death. My silence was now peaceful as I lay there in the dark; alone, only the moon keeping me company in its spherical silence. I refused to sleep. I had to remain awake in case she came out of her silence. I was still hopeful that she would wake up to my songs, my prayers, to our life together in my house in Michigan, surrounded by beautiful gardens created by me to overcome each diatribe.

I waited patiently, her body still immobile. I later realized that just as she could not give me her milk under the bridge that terrible night for she was numb with terror of the bombs, she could not wake up to me now. I realized I no longer needed anything from her. I felt free from her, from my wants. I felt free like a bird, no longer constrained by maternal fetters. It was time that I looked at her for who she was: a woman of great strength, beauty and compassion. I had always seen her according to my needs. She gave to me and to everyone, to the poorest, the lonely, all the love she had within. She gave to us what she could, given her tragic circumstances. Like the French say, she did everything *à la foi*, in good faith. Able to see my mother in this new light was of great comfort to me.

The next morning, she was still motionless. I went to the garden and cut a bouquet of forsythia, the only flower similar to our ginestra, which had been a great part of her panorama. I gathered a bunch of violets and made a bouquet for her, as I used to when I was a child. We were preparing for the last breath of her life; I knew the time had come to say goodbye to my newly found mother.

I began to sing softly to her, for I sensed she could still hear. I recited the psalms she had made me memorize for the occasion. Nothing mattered now but being together. Her earthly journey was coming to an end; mine was beginning.

She now lives outside the sphere of time and space; outside this valley of tears, but always in my memory.

Teresa and Angela Renda, passport photo taken before leaving Italy, 1958

www.ingramcontent.com/pod-product-compliance
Lightning Source LLC
Chambersburg PA
CBHW030437010526
44118CB00011B/678